Babyn Yar
Ukrainian Poets Respond

Ukrainian Research Institute
Harvard University

Harvard Library of Ukrainian Literature 4

Cambridge, Massachusetts

Babyn Yar

Ukrainian Poets Respond

Edited with introduction by
Ostap Kin

Translated by
John Hennessy and Ostap Kin

HURI

Distributed by Harvard University Press
for the Ukrainian Research Institute
Harvard University

The Harvard Ukrainian Research Institute was established in 1973 as an integral part of Harvard University. It supports research associates and visiting scholars who are engaged in projects concerned with all aspects of Ukrainian studies. The Institute also works in close cooperation with the Committee on Ukrainian Studies, which supervises and coordinates the teaching of Ukrainian history, language, and literature at Harvard University.

Printed in India on acid-free paper

ISBN 9780674275591 (hardcover), 9780674271692 (paperback), 9780674271722 (epub), 9780674271739 (PDF)

Library of Congress Control Number: 2021949031

LC record available at https://lccn.loc.gov/2021949031

Cover image: Vasyl′ Ovchynnykov. Pam'iat′ (Memory), ca. 1941–1945. Central State Archive Museum of Literature and Arts of Ukraine. Fond 727, op. 1, od. zb. 3, ark. 2.

Book and cover design by Mykola Leonovych, https://smalta.pro

Publication of this book has been made possible by the Ukrainian Research Institute Fund and the generous support of publications in Ukrainian studies at Harvard University by the following benefactors:

Ostap and Ursula Balaban
Jaroslaw and Olha Duzey
Vladimir Jurkowsky
Myroslav and Irene Koltunik
Damian Korduba Family
Peter and Emily Kulyk
Irena Lubchak
Dr. Evhen Omelsky
Eugene and Nila Steckiw
Dr. Omeljan and Iryna Wolynec
Wasyl and Natalia Yerega

Зміст

Передмова

Поезії

Contents

Introduction

Poems

A Note on Transliteration

The names of people and places in this book have been transliterated according to a modified Library of Congress system, with ligatures are omitted and the й transliterated without the breve, as i rather than ĭ. The Ukrainian apostrophe has been retained. Well-known personal names appear in spellings widely adopted in English-language texts, while the spelling of several other names of living authors follows their own preference or the established use in English, where applicable.

Toponyms are transliterated from the language of the state in which their referent currently lies, thus Lviv, not Lwów or Lvov. In some cases, countries have established an official place-name in the Latin alphabet: Kyiv is one such place (rather than the Library of Congress transliteration *Kyïv*). Where cities have well-established English-language forms, irrespective of alphabet, English-language forms are used. These places include Moscow (not *Moskva*), Warsaw (not *Warszawa*), Vienna (not *Wien*). For rivers that cross international borders, an English-language form also is used, with the exception of the Dnipro instead of Dnieper as it is used in individual poems.

Acknowledgments

First and foremost, I am deeply grateful to John Hennessy for agreeing to embark on this project in the summer of 2020 amidst the global pandemic. I am also thankful to John for providing valuable feedback on other manuscript parts.

I want to express my gratitude to the Editorial Board of the Ukrainian Research Institute, Harvard University, for their decision to pursue the publication of this volume. I also want to thank Oleh Kotsyuba for enthusiastically embracing the idea and spearheading this book project. Special thanks to Michelle Viise for editing the manuscript. I thank two anonymous readers for their helpful feedback on the manuscript.

I owe thanks to the interlibrary loan departments at Rutgers University Libraries and the Mina Rees Library at The Graduate Center, City University of New York, for their assistance with obtaining hard-to-find publications. I, too, would like to thank Ol′ha Odihieieva from the National University Kyiv-Mohyla Academy Library for her assistance.

Oleksandr Boron´ helped substantially with access to some publications and provided editorial advice. Oleksandr Averbuch, too, gave access to rare publications during the lockdown and aided in establishing contact with some heirs. Yohanan Petrovsky-Shtern graciously suggested how to get in touch with several heirs and shared materials I could not otherwise gain access to. Additionally, thanks are due to Aleksandr Anin, Valeriia Bohuslavs´ka, Olena Dobrovol´s´ka, Lev Fridman, Serhii Hirik, Tetiana Teren, Eleonora Solovei, Olena O'Lir, Sergej Parkhomenko, Stanislav Tsalyk, and Liudmyla Zabarylo.

Mykola Zhulyns´kyi and staff of the T. H. Shevchenko Institute of Literature, along with Olena Chyzhova and Ihor Reznik at the Central State Archives Museum of Literature and Arts of Ukraine, aided with locating and sharing images and artworks from their special collections; I would like to thank them for that.

I owe a debt of gratitude to the poets for their permission to include their works. Special thanks go to copyright holders for their permission as well. Every effort has been made to contact all of them—any omissions will be altered in future editions.

Lastly, thank you to Polina Barskova for her constant encouragement and support.

Introduction

Babyn Yar in Ukrainian Poetry

Ostap Kin

Сьогодні одвідав Бабий яр. Жах
Today I visited Babyn Yar. Horror.[1]
– Oleksandr Dovzhenko, 1943

What Happened in the City?

Between the end of World War II and the independence of Ukraine in 1991, the Soviet government launched a number of initiatives, most of them unrealized, to commemorate the massacres at Babyn Yar. The nationality and ethnicity of the victims was always elided under the category of "Kyivans" or "Soviet citizens," and the weak attempts at memorializing the murders took a backseat to plans to obliterate the site altogether by filling the ravine and quarry with industrial wastewater and smoothing the pit over at street level. In 1966 the first marker—a granite stone—was finally erected, and in 1976 a bronze sculpture was installed. Neither memorial mentioned the Jewish identity of the victims of Babyn Yar. It was only in 1991 that Babyn Yar was characterized in Ukraine as a Jewish massacre. A bronze menorah was erected in that year. The cornerstone of a museum was laid in 2001 but no construction followed.[2] In the spring of 2020, almost eighty years after the Babyn Yar massacre in Kyiv, the Ukrainian capital witnessed yet another attempt to create a memorial that would adequately commemorate those who perished; on October 6, 2021, the Foundation and Babyn Yar Holocaust Memorial Center was inaugurated.

During World War II, Babyn Yar was the site of one of the most horrendous massacres in the twentieth century and was central to the "Holocaust by bullets."[3] The Soviet army retreated from Kyiv on September 17, 1941. Nazi troops marched into the city in the early morning of September 19, 1941, marking the beginning of a new epoch in the life of the city and its inhabitants.[4] The Red Army recaptured Kyiv on November 6, 1943, but they arrived in what was an unrecognizable metropolis. The Nazi occupation had utterly changed the architectural, spatial, and intellectual shape of the city.

The most vulnerable part of Kyiv's population proved to be the local Jews. Many of them were unable to leave before the Nazis arrived. On September 28, 1941, around 2,000 copies of the notorious unsigned trilingual announcement, in Russian, Ukrainian, and German, were widely posted across the city. The announcement ordered the Jews of the city to gather on the intersection of two streets by the cemetery. One inhabitant noted in her diary on September 28:

> In the middle of the day, a terrible order for the Jews was posted: that tomorrow, September 29, all of them should gather at eight in the morning at Luk'ianivka (at Babyn Yar) with documents, warm clothes. Those who do not show up will be executed. [...] The distress among the Jews is terrible. It is so hard to look at the suffering of others. Many of them think they will die.[5]

No one really knew the meaning of that order. Some thought the Jews would be sent to the Soviet Union. Others heard they would be relocated to Palestine.[6] Between September 29 and 30, 33,771 Jews were machine-gunned in a ravine on the outskirts of Kyiv. On September 30, the Kyivites already knew what fate had awaited their neighbors: "We found out that the Jews were killed in Babyn Yar. No one expected it."[7] The killings went on, and in the course of Kyiv's Nazi occupation between 100,000 and 150,000 perished in Babyn Yar, most of them Jews. Others killed included patients from psychiatric institutions, representatives of other nationalities inhabiting the city (Ukrainians, Russians, and several Romany camps), Soviet prisoners of war, detained partisans, sailors, members of the Ukrainian nationalist movement, Communists, and others.

Kyiv as a Jewish City

The first Jewish settlements in Kyiv appeared in the earliest years when it was the capital of Kyivan Rus'. The Principality of Lithuania expelled the Mongols in the fifteenth century and the Jews shortly thereafter, but the

Jewish community was quickly reestablished. Another expulsion of the local Jews took place under the rule of Tsar Nicholas I in 1835. However, two of decades later, during the rule of Alexander II, some Jewish groups were again permitted to settle in Kyiv. Between 1859 and 1881, the Jewish community became a significant economic force and made up three-quarters of the first-guild merchants. By the mid-1890s, Jews represented half of all the merchants in the city. After 1881, local Jews were very much involved in organizing Kyiv's rabbinate, as well as hospitals, schools, and synagogues. Beginning in 1905, Jews participated in the formation of political organizations and later began to play a role in the political life of the city.[8]

Before the 1917 revolution, there were more than fifty thousand Jewish residents in the city, constituting some ten percent of the population. These numbers steadily increased over the next two decades. After the Bolsheviks took power in Kyiv, they began to control all Jewish institutions and soon closed some of them. In 1926, the number of Jews was 140,256, which was 27 percent of the total population of Kyiv. On the eve of the war, according to the 1939 census, the total population of the city was 846,724 residents[9]; Jews constituted 26.5 percent of the population, or 224,236 people.[10]

How "Poetry about Babyn Yar" Is Organized

Today, Ukrainians—shaped and tested by a variety of political and historical events—are still looking for ways to understand the tragedy of the Holocaust in Ukraine. The question of Ukrainian complicity in the Holocaust in general and in the tragedy of Babyn Yar in particular is a broad and important one. A number of important historical studies, monographs, and academic volumes, have been published on these topics.[11] In most cases, these works are based on documents from archives and special collections and they use eyewitness accounts to build a narrative.

There are other media that might help us understand the tragedy of the Holocaust more broadly and the tragedy of Babyn Yar specifically. One such medium is the poems written in response to the massacre. Poetry is an extremely reactive form of art; it can present an emotional and immediate response to an event, often before any deliberation or reworking to fit political narratives. Therefore, it can serve to measure people's reactions and emotions—compassion, understanding, lack of empathy, or even an unwillingness to tell the truth.[12]

This anthology presents a number of responses to the events in Babyn Yar created in the years 1941–2018, that is, in the course of several historical phases and artistic movements in Soviet and post-Soviet Ukraine.[13] Poets belonging to distinct literary traditions and political epochs responded to the tragedy; this collection attempts to create a catalog of those reactions. Of particular interest is the publication history of these texts. The poems collected here were at times excluded from the poets' subsequent selected or collected editions, meaning that they remained unread. Publishing was tightly controlled by the state at every stage, requiring ideological and artistic compliance from writers. This raises the question about the interaction between the Soviet poet and the censor, especially in the case of writing about the Holocaust; the poems that emerge out of such interactions must be read with an understanding of the explicit and implicit censorship to which the authors were subject. The limitations imposed by censorship and self-censorship can often be felt in the details of the poems dedicated to the Holocaust.

The poems featured in this book can be divided into three periods, although these periods also have their subdivisions. The first includes the years 1941–46, the time of the Nazi occupation as well as the period after Kyiv was recaptured by the Soviet army. The poems from this period may, in turn, be divided into at least three more categories: (a) works created by someone who lived in the city during the Nazi occupation and witnessed the events (a number of inhabitants left their diaries); (b) the 1942 responses to the Nazi atrocities by the Soviet Ukrainian poets who escaped Ukraine during the evacuation (such influential names in Ukrainian literature as Pavlo Tychyna, Maksym Ryl′s′kyi, and Volodymyr Sosiura); and c) poems composed by poets who returned to or visited the city after it was recaptured by the Red Army in 1943 (Mykola Bazhan and Volodymyr Sosiura, as well as two younger poets who had just come of age at that time: Vasyl′ Shvets′ and Oleksa Iushchenko).[14]

Following the five years after Kyiv was retaken from the Nazis the harsh period of 1948–49 and the 1950s began, an enormously difficult phase in the history of Ukrainian Jewry, when a large number of Ukrainian Jews in the literary field were publicly disparaged and humiliated in the press and endured severe pressure as part of a ferocious state-orchestrated anti-Semitic campaign. Many topics related to Babyn Yar simply ceased to be published for more than a decade. The poems from this second period began appearing in the early 1960s, partially coinciding with the twentieth and twenty-fifth anniversaries of the mass killings. Of special note here is the publication of Anatolii Kuznetsov's novel *Babii Iar: roman-dokument* (Babi Yar: A document in the form of a novel; 1966 and 1967) and Yevgeny Yevtushenko's poem "Babi Yar" (1961). Extensive public controversies and discussions surrounded these publications.[15] The second period lasted, again very roughly, through the 1970s until *perestroika* (1980s) and the collapse of the Soviet Union in 1991. The number of authors who published in this second period is rather large and includes mainly official poets. This category of poet includes, on the one hand, the modernist poet Leonid Pervomais′kyi, who began his literary career in the late 1920s, and, on the other hand, the poets who emerged and began to write in the 1950s, 1960s, and 1970s, and who might be dubbed the second wave of Ukrainian Soviet modernism. (Here, the poems of Ivan Drach and Moisei Fishbein are especially intriguing.) This period also includes poets who were not engaged in building a bridge between the early and later movements of Ukrainian modernism (the one interrupted in the 1930s by political repressions and restarted in a clandestine manner in the 1960s). These "non-modernist" poets are interesting for one reason: they demonstrate the official, conformist, censor-approved writing that was permitted to appear in print. As the scholar Ilya Kukulin noted:

> One of the characteristic features of Soviet poetry, especially the poetry of war, was its teleological tendency. The image of a given (or implied) socially valuable aim—such as victory in the war, or the establishment of communism, or progress of society—was a counterweight to pain, or hunger, or the necessity of suffering. In Soviet literature, the hope for a better future gave meaning to any social conflicts and existential problems.[16]

For that reason, a poem by Marta Tarnawsky—written in emigration—differs tremendously from what was written at that time in the Soviet Union. Tarnawsky, first of all, establishes a direct link with the Ukrainian modernist literature repressed by the authorities; living abroad, she was free to do so openly while her counterparts in the Soviet Ukraine were not as fortunate. Secondly, she was able to write freely about the childhood traumas of the Holocaust experienced in Galicia (a part of what is now western Ukraine), something quite unimaginable in the Ukraine of the 1970s.

The third period began on the eve of the collapse of the Soviet Union and accelerated after the independence of Ukraine. A new era had arrived: poets were freed from fear of the state and its censors and the suffocating political atmosphere of the Soviet Union. These political developments opened the doors to the introduction of new stylistic approaches and allowed discussion of Babyn Yar in a way markedly different from that of the past. Vivid creations by Ukrainian Jewish poets appear: Hryhorii Fal´kovych, Abram Katsnel´son, Arkadii Anin and, much later, Denys Holubyts´kyi, are published. The culmination of this period is marked by the publication of

Marianna Kiyanovska's award-winning collection *Babyn Iar: Holosamy* (The voices of Babyn Yar; 2017). In it, Kiyanovska offers a fresh and hitherto little-used method of approaching the victims by performing their voices; in other words, she looks at the city and its catastrophe through the eyes of its Jewish inhabitants. In her poetry, the victims are given voices to tell their stories. While they may call to mind eyewitness accounts recorded years after the event took place, Kiyanovska's subjects are not being interviewed or recorded years later. It is as if they share their stories right after the event, or as the events are unfolding—as if their voices have survived in order to relate the gruesome experiences they have gone through. The poet is relying not only on the tradition of Ukrainian modernism but also the radical methods offered by various other European modernisms. By applying those approaches to her confessional writing, Kiyanovska is able to construct a persuasive narrative, a wide palette of emotions, and, even more importantly, to give voices to the anonymous victims.

Two years after the massacre at Babyn Yar happened, the Polish poet Czesław Miłosz wrote a poem entitled "A Poor Christian Looks at the Ghetto":

> Bees build around the honeycomb of lungs,
> Ants build around white bone.
> Torn is paper, rubber, linen, leather, flax,
> Fiber, fabrics, cellulose, snakeskin, wire.
> The roof and the wall collapse in flame
>   and heat seizes the foundations.
> Now there is only the earth, sandy, trodden down,
> With one leafless tree.

> Slowly, boring a tunnel, a guardian mole makes his way,
> With a small red lamp fastened to his forehead.
> He touches buried bodies, counts them, pushes on,
> He distinguishes human ashes by their luminous vapor,
> The ashes of each man by a different
>   part of the spectrum.
> [...]
> I am afraid, so afraid of the guardian mole.
> He has swollen eyelids, like a Patriarch
> Who has sat much in the light of candles
> Reading the great book of the species.
> What will I tell him, I, a Jew of the New Testament,
> Waiting two thousand years for the
>   second coming of Jesus?
> My broken body will deliver me to his sight
> And he will count me among the helpers of death:
> The uncircumcised.[17]

In this poem, the poet offers a sharp response to the experiences of war. Miłosz presents the reader with a landscape that has been desolated and whose people were annihilated. The poet's narrator is dead, decomposing. The language that the narrator uses in the verse initiated a much-needed discussion about various modes of remembrance. Similarly, the poems collected in this anthology also invite their readers to a potential dialogue, contemplation, and remembrance. Above all, these poems showcase various efforts at communication with those who perished at Babyn Yar. For many poets, the experience of living in a city where so many people—whole families, friends, foes, neighbors, lovers, colleagues, and just fellow inhabitants—were simply erased presented a confounding paradox. How was one to cope with this city's emptiness and the death of these people? What words can be used to at least broach these events, if not to transmit them? How should one start this conversation with, in, and about the past?

Recreating Memories of the Tragedy

In the Soviet Union, the practices of commemoration took a different form: for the most part, these practices were selective and a number of categories of people were excluded from memory. As Olga Gershenson claims,

> Foremost among the forgotten were the Jews. There was no institution of Holocaust memory within Soviet borders. The word "Holocaust" itself was not used—the particular Jewish loss had no name. There was no clearly formulated, consistent policy regarding the Holocaust; instead, beginning in 1943, the tendency was to silence any discussion of the matter. Although this vague policy and its enforcement fluctuated over the time. . .throughout most of the Soviet era the silencing mechanism remained the same: the Holocaust was not denied, it just was not treated as a unique separate phenomenon. The Holocaust was, instead, generally universalized by subsuming it as part of the overall Soviet tragedy, with Jews euphemistically labeled "peaceful Soviet citizens."[18]

Shortly after the end of World War II, the Soviets abandoned any initial ideas to properly commemorate the Jewish victims in Babyn Yar and decided instead to focus on commemorating the Soviet people. The reasons for doing so, Timothy Snyder argued, were as follows:

> For the Soviet authorities the memory of the Holocaust was not useful. Because it would reveal the fact that Nazism is not just a form of fascism against communism, but also a force against Jews. Therefore, for the Soviet authorities, it was inconvenient to confirm that Jews had suffered more than other parts of Soviet society. That is why, from the very beginning and later, the Soviet authorities did not portray the Babi Yar massacre as mainly a tragedy of Jews.[19]

The Red Army retook Kyiv only in 1943, when in the early morning of November 6 Soviet troops rushed into the city. Nikita Khrushchev, the future leader of the Soviet Union, headed to Kyiv accompanied by three writers. The writers were meant to describe what they saw, though their written impressions were originally aimed at several different audiences and had a number of ideological goals. After he entered the city, the writer Iurii Ianovs´kyi observed in a published piece:

> On November 6, 1943, Kyiv was a desert—the Germans got rid of all Kyivites. Some buildings were still in flames, set on fire by the enemy during the night of their retreat. Khreshchatyk lay in ruins . . .[However,] Kyiv was recognizable... Kyiv breathed and lived. In the clouds of dust and smoke, which hovered above the streets, a living city smiled at us. This smile was painful, tears of happiness ran down its cheeks. The first day of freedom after two years of German torture had begun. Solitary Kyivans started leaving their shelters.[20]

His report aims to capture the devastating conditions the city had been enduring, and its sigh of relief after the Red Army troops finally marched into the city. Following the tradition of socialist realism, the author gives this city a chance to smile painfully and cry tears of happiness.

Oleksandr Dovzhenko had been jotting down events in his private diary in a similar way: "[A]round noon [on November 6, 1943], N[ikita] Khrushchev, Marshal Zhukov, and I went to Kyiv. Destroyed roads, dead animals, in one word, everything is as if at war. We entered Kyiv from the side of Kurenivka, Podil, headed to Khreshchatyk. Khreshchatyk was on fire."[21] He then proceeded to describe the city:

> The more I look at Kyiv, the more I see what a great tragedy Kyiv has endured. There is actually no population in Kyiv. There is a small group of poor, needy, impoverished survivors. There are no children, no young men or women. Only old women and disabled people. This is a stunning picture. Our world hasn't seen anything like this in the course of a few centuries, of many centuries. Because Kyiv was a city of millions. Now, among the ruins there are fifty thousand.[22]

Although the architectural collapse of the city was an enormously painful thing to experience and endure, it was the city dwellers, or, to be more precise, the lack thereof, that impressed the writer the most:

> What struck me the most, plunged me into unforgettable sorrow and despair and longing which I also never forgot were the people. The Kyiv people. They weren't there. The city was empty. I saw only around a hundred of them alone or in small groups. These were largely the old, those with war injuries, or the disabled. But all of them had that mad look that one can never forget. They were semi-insane, thin, skinny,

> and yellow, with unnatural hysterical movements and wide unhealthy eyes.[23]

Describing this sight in great detail becomes a crucial theme for a diverse group of poets for several generations. From what is known, there are no poems written by survivors of the massacre in the ravine, although we do have a number of testimonies that are, of course, a source of valuable material.

No matter how gruesome the panorama was and how desperate the inhabitants were, a new cycle of life and history had begun. Shortly thereafter, an influx of people arrived in the city and merged with those who stayed there through the occupation. Very soon it became clear that the people needed art to be able to talk and think about their war experiences. This means that a special place was reserved for poetry by the war survivors and it played the role of a healing, interpreting medium ready to assist with daily reminiscences of horrific wartime experiences. The poet Evdokiia Ol´shanskaia reminisced that in 1945 Kyiv was in dire need of what is now called Holocaust poetry. Specifically, she discusses how the inhabitants consumed Il´ia Sel´vinskii's renowned poem "I Saw It!" about a massacre of Jews near Kerch in an anti-tank ditch:

> She [the poet's sister] sent me poems she liked. Once she sent me a poem by Ilya Selvinsky. It was called "I Saw It!" It told about the execution of Jews in Crimea. But Kievans received it as a description of the tragedy of Babi Yar. . . . Therefore in Kiev the poem "I Saw It!" was passed from hand to hand, people copied it, memorized it, which is how it had reached me.[24]

Poets were on the frontline of those who produced artistic responses to the mass annihilation of Jews in the Soviet Union, and they wrote their poems in Russian, Yiddish, or Ukrainian.[25]

Bazhan and the Poems of Sights

Mykola Bazhan was among those first three Ukrainian writers who entered the city of Kyiv right after it was recaptured by the Red Army. His impressions of what he observed in the city were akin to those depicted by his peers: the panoramas of houses buried in ruins, still in flames. In addition to that, it was difficult to maneuver between the shattered buildings. The images of those destroyed edifices and what they were like during the poet's life in the city began to merge and intertwine in the poet's mind. In his description, while walking the city, the poet barely notices any people on the streets until this unexpected encounter in the center of the city:

> Two figures were running down towards us. A woman and a man. They waved their hands, shouted something indistinctly, either cried or laughed, they threw themselves onto us to hug. The man embraced me. . . . "You are Bazhan, you are Bazhan!" the man kept repeating. I could smell his horrible and deadly stench. He smelled of soot, ashes, decay, sweat and dirty body and of that eerie spirit which smells close to insanity, which blows from the mentally ill. "Don't you recognize me? I'm Shul´man, an artist from the first cinema," the man is telling me hurriedly, hurrying and being nervous that I don't recognize him. My God, even if I remembered the artist from the first cinema, would it be possible to recognize

> anyone in this pitiful, thin, pale and almost crazy creature who came seeking warmth, friendship, and companionship? . . .He calmed down a bit and told us his story. Since October 1941 he had been sitting for two years, or rather standing, in a large masonry stove in their apartment where he arranged a hiding place by removing bricks. His wife, a Ukrainian, let him go out from this depressing cell only at night. Wearing socks so that his neighbors wouldn't hear him, he walked around the room and kneaded his frozen body. His wife started working somewhere, brought a pitiful ration, fed her husband. This lasted for two years. When Shul´man saw us, these were his first steps under a long-unseen sky, even though it was gloomy, even though it was windy with wet snow, it was his hometown, it was free, and it was his.[26]

In a chance meeting with Shul´man, one of a small number of Kyiv Jews to survive Babyn Yar, Bazhan faces for the first time the decimated part of Kyiv's inhabitants—its Jewish part, which constituted approximately twenty-five percent of the capital's prewar population. Shortly thereafter, a visit to the site of the mass killing of the Kyiv Jews triggered the creation of one of the first, and most gripping, responses to the tragedy: "Ravine."[27]

Not only was it a personal reflection on historical events but, in fact, also a nuanced report—a diligent work of a careful-minded reporter, if not an inspector, who observes the place after being summoned there. Bazhan's poem already features an approximation of the total number of victims who perished on site—something that was known more or less immediately ("a desperate cry of one hundred thousand hearts" or "the traces of one hundred thousand"). The poem also reconstructs the overall panorama of the site and describes the remnants of people who ended up here, producing a strong emotional response in the reader: "Silver dust of burnt bones. / A cracked piece of human forehead." Or: "And smoldering, thrown to the side, / A child's shoe covered in blood" goes along with "the broken lens of an old man's glasses." Was it an attempt at a journalistic account from the site? Or should we consider this a poet's imagination? We do know of some details from the writer Oleksii Poltorats´kyi, who visited the site and later told an American reporter: "I went out to Babi Yar shortly after the war was over. As I walked along I tripped over the torn shoe of a little child. I have never gone back there since."[28] In "Ravine," after the description of the place and people, the poet slowly pans his imaginary camera and over to the flames and smoke that mark death during the Holocaust. Here Bazhan includes the surviving inhabitants who by chance witnessed the events: "And people saw from their mournful shelters" how "flesh and blood were brutally burned." Bazhan's poem, written in a baroque language that instantly recalls his oeuvre of the late 1920s and early 1930s, might be considered a point where new poetry of trauma, the poetry of the Holocaust composed in Ukrainian, began. Though written in a politically and ideologically charged atmosphere, it nonetheless contains some of the clearest evidence of the poet's mastery, which did not vanish in spite of the horrendous ideological aura that permeated the late 1930s.

Drach and the Atmosphere of the Year 1966

Yohanan Petrovsky-Shtern puts particular emphasis on the commemorative events that took place on September 29, 1966, in Kyiv's Babyn Yar, as well as on what happened before or after that day, as a paradigm-shifting moment in the history of Ukrainians and Jews. The decade after the war passed in a careful silence enforced by the state-organized anti-Semitic campaigns of the late 1940s and the early 1950s, but the decade of the 1960s brought significant changes. On the day commemorating the twenty-fifth anniversary of the mass killings, between five and twelve hundred people gathered on the site. Participants included the Ukrainian writers Ivan Dziuba and Borys Antonenko-Davydovych, as well as the Russian writer Viktor Nekrasov. Someone asked Dziuba to say a few words. Without having notes at hand, Dziuba spontaneously delivered a speech, which he jotted down after coming home.[29] In it, the literary scholar said:

> Today I want to say a few words here—a thousandth part of what I am thinking and what I would like to say. I want to address you as people—as my brothers and fellow humans. I want to address you, Jews, as a Ukrainian, as a member of the Ukrainian nation to which I proudly belong. Babyn Yar is a tragedy of all mankind, but it took place on Ukrainian soil. Therefore, a Ukrainian, like a Jew, does not have the right to forget it. Babyn Yar is our joint tragedy, a tragedy first and foremost of the Jewish and Ukrainian peoples.[30]

The importance of that commemorative event cannot be underestimated, as cannot the writings on Babyn Yar by Leonid Pervomais´kyi in 1964, and Leonid Cherevatenko and Ivan Drach in 1966.

An article on Babyn Yar in *The New York Times* from the same year points out the feelings of Soviet contemporary times and the sense of forgetting that indisputably prevailed over that of commemorating and remembering on the official level. A reporter for the newspaper vividly portrays a Soviet-style paradise erected on the outskirts of the city, where memories of the gruesome past do not appear to be in high demand. The report conveys the atmosphere of the district in the following way:

> Connecting with the main trolley route, No. 56 bus turned into Demyan Bedny Street. On the right were rows of five-story apartment houses with groceries and little repair shops on the ground floor. On the left was Babi Yar. . . . Now couples who have no memories of the war stroll through the wooded fringes. Neighborhood boys have staked out two soccer fields. A small girl with a big red bow in her hair made mudpies on the sidelines. . . . The boys ended their soccer game as night fell. The strollers went to their homes. Behind their modern apartment building there was a lovely pink sunset, but on the ground that was Babi Yar darkness came quickly.[31]

This portrayal of a Soviet-style amnesiac idyll is astonishing and truthful. The site, while as notorious as Buchenwald or Auschwitz in the West, was given little import in Soviet Ukraine. In the same year the poet Ivan Drach published a poem that on the surface treated the subject similarly. However, Drach differed from a Western reporter who had the freedom to write whatever was actually on their mind; the Soviet Ukrainian poet could not be so overt. Whatever he wrote, he would not be able to discredit the homegrown paradise of the Soviet Union. Drach's poem offers a Brueghel-like portrait of an intense, yet tranquil and joyful, Soviet existence playing out right in the middle of the site of the tragedy. Most people are calm and relaxed, while only an elderly woman is agitated and wishes to sell crosses to the inhabitants. Some mysterious and loud heavy machinery undermines this otherwise idyllic picture of life.

> somewhere pile drivers pounded firm ground
> and someone shoveled sky over me
> firm with the roots of clouds
>   with stones of sun
> so that the metal cobras of lanterns
> hid their long necks in brushwood (85)

The imagery forms a recurring theme in this collection: memories or visions of the past are gained not through working with facts but through dreams.

Kiyanovska and the New Style of Performative Witnessing

Kiyanovska's poems are written in a deliberately colloquial language as though the speakers (the survivors as well as the dead) were summoned by some invisible divine power and invited to provide their eyewitness accounts of the events. Thus, here they are: their language is broken, unpunctuated, their thoughts are scattered, and their emotions are heightened. In her poems, several utterances remain opaque to the reader. These are thoughts that remain unfinished. At times, these poems resemble a transcript of conversations that were not edited, clarified, or polished, which makes the verses so powerful. The unedited voices, transcribed word by word, contain painful emotions and convey the overall atmosphere of the period, as when a character says, "unusual things in my suitcase i've packed / the way people pack for the road these days / only the key letters photographs a brooch and money / all right not exactly money just a few bills."

Kiyanovska's poetry is exemplary in that it deals with ordinary things that are the sources of feelings and emotions, the things that could help reproduce the fragments of memory: a school diary, a notebook, letters, and even herbaria. Forgotten and dumped in the remote corner of one's attic, in reality, these are the only lines capable of reconnecting one with the past, loved ones, relatives, or neighbors. This collection of everyday objects is a link to traumatic memories as well, which one might be very much willing to get rid of.

The Key Tropes

A good deal of attention in the poetic responses to the massacre is given to Babyn Yar as a site, the scene of the killings, and as a place serving as a grave for all those murdered here. Equally, the places that are located around the site are described in both the early and later poetry. The geographical locations of that part of Kyiv serve a purpose: they are often inhabited by witnesses to the atrocities:

> And people saw from their mournful shelters
> How beyond the crowns of Kyryliv's buildings
> Beyond the poplars of distant cemeteries,
> Their flesh and blood were brutally burned
> (Bazhan, 1943, 55)

The city's district of Podil, known for its sizeable number of Jewish residents, became a place full of fear:

> But where did the air go
> that filled lungs with the night
> in the room at the first cry, so much screaming
> over Podil, over all of Kyiv
> (Shvets´, 1944, 195)

Later, other poets introduced key geographical locations, notorious as places where the Jews gathered or moved through on the way to their deaths. More prominently, one of Kyiv's streets—Melnyk Street—stands out in particular. Sava Holovanivs´kyi reconstructs the ordeal Jews had to endure while marching down Melnyk Street. As the street undergoes a reconstruction, modernization, and upgrades, it also loses its quality as a direct witness of the crime, and so it is being stripped of its memory, its value as a witness. As a place, it will no longer be able to offer to future generations something it possesses at this particular point:

Let the young people walk along here
and sometimes trip over potholes
lest they forget the terror of those times,
the columns of the condemned and despairing!

(1975, 115)

In his emotional verses Holovanivs′kyi relies on the 19th-century romantic tradition of poetry, while Dabo-Nikolaiev offers an experimental modernist take that introduces sound as a companion to the narrator in his poem:

swoosh
of shoe-bottoms
from Halytska square
westward
to the Sun
like anthracite
to Babyn
Yar

(2001, 81)

Beside geographical localization of the tragedy, another crucial trope is that of vengeance. This trope is especially strong in the earliest poems, when the creative moment immediately follows the experience of seeing the city of Kyiv upon the poets' arrival with the Red Army, or their discovery of the tragedy. However, even in 1942, before the poets themselves followed the Red Army troops into the city, there were poetic appeals to justice on behalf of the victims. For instance, Pavlo Tychyna mentions both

European ghettos and the revenge that will fall on the German perpetrators:

> Let our wrath boil, ignite like a thunderstorm,
> the unthinkable ghettos in Europe! Let the Germans
> know there will be vengeance:—Halt!
> (1942, 223)

Especially eloquent in demanding retribution is Volodymyr Sosiura, whose calls can be followed through the years. Sosiura, who had been evacuated from Kyiv, sent a poem to be read at a Jewish rally in Ufa in September 1942[32]:

> We'll drive the beast together into the abyss,
> we'll scatter the black ashes of brownshirt hordes,
> because we love our native land beyond measure (**201**)

He wrote another poem in 1943, most likely after returning to Kyiv and visiting the site:

> We'll find everyone who spilled the blood of children,
> who left the horrendous rows of
> corpses in ravines (209)

In mourning the deaths of children and calling for them to be avenged, poets invoke the biblical figure of Rachel. Pavlo Tychyna, for example, proclaims:

> We hear the keening from Europe: Rakhil
> mourning for her children, a mother's
> lament... O, these tears and pain

will resound through centuries, an accusation
against their silence!
(223)

The Soviet censor compels Tychyna to obscure the origin of the lament; the weeping of Tychyna's Rachel can be heard in Europe, not in Ukraine. Yet this seems to be a displacement of Jewish suffering that is perhaps the only way for Tychyna to indicate what was happening to the Jews of Ukraine, substituting their plight with that of the Jews of Europe, as Soviet state ideology demanded. Several poets invoke the names of those who perished, thus lending their calls for revenge and justice additional power. Lina Kostenko names all the victims lying in the ravine outside the city, an act that enables her to treat the loss as real rather than symbolic. She commemorates a long, inclusive list of the deceased:

People say: everyone was buried alive
Somewhere here in the valley.
Here, Odarka, a watchful mother,
Peacemaker in children's fights.
Here Lavrin, known for proverbs,
And Kryvenko, a gray-haired shoemaker.
Here Iurko, and Khana with dark eyes,
All my little friends.
Here's the soil; it has a deep wound,
Don't touch it, it hurts the soil.[33]

The most radical approach in this regard has been offered recently by Marianna Kiyanovska. The title of her collection juxtaposes two things: the names we give Babyn Yar and the voices that evoke the lives of the victims. In one of the poems, we encounter a woman sharing her story. As she finishes, she sums it all up by uttering her name, Rakhel, as the last word of the poem:

> and now i'm leaving for good i understand and see
> all our doom through the glitter of intense lights
> i would die on this street and so i don't cry
> but i settle my suitcase on cobblestones
>   i carry only my name
> i'm rakhel (143)

There is also the story of a schoolboy who has miraculously survived and is now hiding with his other surviving classmate, Srulik. Once, Srulik punched the speaker in the face, but that does not matter at this point:

> srulik punched me i would have even forgotten about it
> if not for the fact that he and i
> miraculously survived out of the whole class (145)

Finally, the speaker names the Nazis committing the atrocities:

> here is the ravine where hans does his shooting
> (...)
> but kuno is spitting out another round and laughter
> here is fritz near rivka some three wounds but
> (...)
> rivka hears everything even the heartbeat
> fritz shoots her in the belly and says: garbage
> here is albert brother of the murdered yona a jew
> (...).

> here is young miriam who was happy
> here she is being embraced by poor small
> dead tsylia who warms her up with
>   warmth without warmth (155)

Naming gives reality to the victims and perpetrators alike.

Probably one of the most intriguing aspects of the poems collected in this volume is their language. In some, we see the prescribed Soviet style of writing about a catastrophe, while others are written in the freer language we encounter in the post-Soviet period. Dealing with trauma requires an instrument of particular subtlety, and language is one such instrument. Was the poetic language that existed in Soviet Ukraine before World War II capable of transmitting an honest emotional response to catastrophe, or was a new language necessary, a language unencumbered by the pathos and didacticism of socialist realism? Although there were many historical events that could have propelled the emergence of such a language—World War I and its aftermath, the 1917–1921 political and military struggles in Ukraine, the Holodomor and its aftermath, the Gulag experiences throughout the 1930s, and the 1986 Chernobyl tragedy—it was largely impossible to write and publish genuine responses in the Soviet political atmosphere and with the ideological restrictions it imposed: the consequences for the poet would have begun with a prison sentence.[34]

Another aspect of this challenge was the need to construct a new language after the Holocaust took place on the territories of the Soviet Union occupied by the Nazis. Therefore, the poems collected in this anthology showcase a language or, rather, languages capable of portraying suffering such as that endured at Babyn Yar. It was a striking experience to put together these unconnected poems, composed in different decades following the war, and to find a sense of trauma permeating them in different ways—trauma that was in search of tools to express it, whether within the boundaries of the existing (Soviet) Ukrainian language, or outside of them.

Previous Collections

In order to compile this anthology, I worked predominantly with first editions, the sources in which the individual poems were first published, from newspapers to single-author collections. Not surprisingly, a number of poems were published in outlets that are hard to locate today. Some were featured only in newspapers and never reprinted.[35] A particular challenge of compiling an anthology such as this one lay in its goal to be representative of a wide range of poetry in terms of style and viewpoint, while also summarizing eight decades of writing about Babyn Yar. As Amir Weiner argued,

> The mass murder of Jews was never denied in Soviet representations of the war, but in the official accounts and artistic representations, memory of the Jewish catastrophe was submerged within the universal Soviet tragedy, erasing the very distinction at the core of the Nazi pursuit of racial purity.[36]

While an anthology dedicated to Babyn Yar wouldn't have been permitted during the Soviet era, individual poems about Babyn Yar were published.[37] The most active period began with *perestroika*, when censorship was relaxed. This period also saw the publication of anthologies of poems dedicated to Babyn Yar in Ukraine. Beginning in 1991, Iurii Kaplan, a Ukrainian Kyiv-based Russophone poet, was actively involved in publishing books on the Babyn Yar tragedy. He prepared for publication as many as three different editions of a poetry collection. The first, entitled in the Russian language *Ekho Bab′ego Iara* (The Echo of Babyn Yar), appeared in 1991, in a print run of some fifty thousand copies. This was followed by two subsequent editions, in 2001 and 2006. These anthologies included bilingual presentations of poems written originally in Ukrainian or Russian, as well as translations from Yiddish into Russian. Both came out under the same title in Ukrainian, *Vidlunnia Babynoho Iaru* (The Echo of Babyn Yar). Each new edition included more poems and supplied critical materials by new individuals; the literary scholar Ivan Dziuba wrote an introduction to the second edition, whereas Oleksandr Moroz, the then-head of the Socialist Party of Ukraine, prefaced the third edition and had his original 1982 poem included in the anthology as well. There were also some unexpected additions. For example, Paul Celan's quintessential Holocaust poem "Todesfuge" (Death Fugue) in Vasyl′ Stus's translation and Marina Tsvetaeva's poem "To the Jews" were included in the collection.[38] Apart from the three Kaplan anthologies, there have been other notable attempts to anthologize poetry about Babyn Yar—including the 1991 volume *Bol'* (Pain), edited by the Kyiv-based literary scholar and poet Ritalii Zaslavskii,[39] and the 2004 anthology entitled *Babyn Iar* edited by Il′ia Levitas, another scholar, who edited several books on Babyn Yar.[40] Like Kaplan's, these anthologies included bilingual presentations of poems written originally in Ukrainian and Russian, as well as Yiddish to Russian translations.[41]

Poems related to Babyn Yar appeared now and then in official Soviet publications; they are included here. Clearly, there were poems published in the past that are yet to be found and reprinted. We know about some of them from passing comments in the press of the day. In addition to that, it is fair to assume that there were other poems that were once published but remain beyond the reader's accessibility for various reasons: they appeared in hard-to-find publications, were omitted by scholars or negatively perceived by official critics and therefore were erased not just from the canon but from any literary map. It is also fair to say that every editor will have their own selection of texts in Ukrainian on Babyn Yar, which can only benefit the overall goal of discovery and commentary. However, as of today, there is no authoritative canon of Ukrainian-language poems on Babyn Yar; in fact, no anthology of exclusively Ukrainian-language poems on Babyn Yar has ever been published before. The present bilingual edition is the first such undertaking. This is not entirely surprising, as a project such as this one always remains a work in progress that, in fact, may never be completed. Babyn Yar will remain vivid in Ukrainian letters, and new poems about Babyn Yar will continue to be written.

Our translations were chosen predominantly for their content, though we have done our best to make a selection showcasing a range of formal elements and different styles. Stemming from such different periods, the poems' contrasting styles, diction, and syntax required special attention. Most, if not all of the poems display unexpected linguistic layers and vocabulary, specific local details, and the ever-present atmosphere of the Soviet era. Additionally, we encounter Soviet vs. post-Soviet approaches to versification and formal structures, especially with regard to what one could say overtly. Taken together, the poems presented here posed challenges for the translators tasked with deciphering their meaning and preparing adequate English-language equivalents. As always, the translation process is a constant compromise, an activity where one often has to think about what to keep and what to change, and how to make it sound natural. It hardly needs to be said that translation inevitably requires acts of interpretation.

Instead of a Conclusion

The artist Vasyl´ Ovchynnykov (1907–78) returned to Kyiv after the city was recaptured by the Red Army. His own house was destroyed; however, he was more interested in the fate of his Jewish neighbors:

> He began asking questions about their fate, the artist's daughter later recalled. "The thing is that many neighboring families were Jewish."
>
> "The Zalvalses?"
>
> "Went to Babyn Yar."
>
> "The Knizhniks?"
>
> "In Babyn Yar."

The answer to Ovchynnykov's questions about the fate of other Jewish neighbors was the same: "In Babyn Yar, in Babyn Yar. . ."[42] Shaken by the erasure of so many people and by the cruelty of their execution, Ovchynnykov began work on what would become a triptych in charcoal and sanguine (chalk) chronicling the final days of the Jews of Kyiv at Babyn Yar. Operating under the familiar constraints of official Soviet policy, which prohibited the singling out of Jews as particular victims of the Nazis, the artist nevertheless made very clear that it was the execution of 34,000 Jews on two days in 1941 that his triptych memorialized, naming the first panel "29 September," and showing in three scenes the gathering of Jews in the streets, their forced march to Babyn Yar, and their entrance into the quarry before being commanded to undress. The taboo on identifying victim groups makes it possible to imagine characters to be either witnesses or victims of Nazi persecution. A reporter for the newspaper *Radians´ke mystetstvo* visited Ovchynnykov in his studio, and began his article: "Decades will pass, centuries will pass, but civilized humanity will never forget the tens of thousands of graves where the victims of fascism are buried: millions perished in the German concentration camps, machine-gunned in Kerch, in Babyn Yar, burnt in crematoriums, and choked in gas vans."[43] The newspaper account once again makes clear that even though it was possible to mention several locations where large numbers of Soviet (and European) Jews perished, it was improper to specify that these victims were in fact Jews.

As David Roskies and Naomi Diamant suggest, "Holocaust literature [...] unfolds both backward and forward: backward, as previously unknown works are published, annotated, translated, catalogued, and promptly forgotten; and forward, as new works of ever greater subtlety or simplicity come into being."[44] The poems collected in this volume show that the attempt to understand and commemorate the tragedy of Babyn Yar began in Ukraine almost immediately after the massacre. But this selection of poetry also presses us to uncover more of the variety of ways this horrific moment in history was commemorated and continues to be commemorated in the literature of today.

Notes

1 Oleksandr Dovzhenko, *Shchodennykovi zapysy, 1939–1956 [Dnevnikovye zapisi. 1939–1956]*, edited by V. V. Zabrodin, E. Ia. Margolit (Kharkiv: Folio, 2013), 265. Unless otherwise indicated, all translations from Ukrainian and Russian are mine. An editorial note accompanying this undated Babyn Yar entry specifies that "the bottom part of a page is torn away." Today, it is impossible to establish if that part included the author's further reflections on what he observed on the site. Although this is an undated entry, it was most likely written during the writer's initial visit to the city when it was recaptured, in early November 1943, or shortly thereafter.

2 Karel C. Berkhoff, "Babi Yar: Site of Mass Murder, Ravine of Oblivion," J. B. and Maurice C. Shapiro Annual Lecture, February 9, 2011, 9–13, https://www.ushmm.org/m/pdfs/Publication_OP_2011-02.pdf.

3 On the Holocaust by bullets see Father Patrick Desbois, *The Holocaust by Bullets: A Priest's Journey to Uncover the Truth Behind the Murder of 1.5 Million Jews* (New York: Palgrave Macmillan, 2009).

4 On the daily life of Kyivites during the German occupation, see Karel Berkhoff, *Harvest of Despair: Life and Death in Ukraine Under Nazi Rule* (Cambridge: The Belknap Press of Harvard University Press, 2004).

5 "Shchodennyk Niny Herasymovoï—meshkanky okupovanoho m. Kyïv. 1941–1945." Tsyfrovi kolektsiï Natsional´noho muzeiu istoriï Ukraïny u Druhii svitovii viini. 16 March 2016 https://digital.warmuseum.kiev.ua/documents/9 (accessed May 30, 2021). On Herasymova diary and its possible adaptation later in the 1950s, see: Andrii Portnov, "Viina. Kyïv. Shchodennyk," in Viktoriia Kolosova, *Kyïvs'kyi shchodennyk. 1940–1945*, eds. Olesia

Lazarenko and Andrii Portnov (Kharkiv: Vydavnytstvo "Prava liudyny," 2021), 11–12.

6 A. Anatoli (Kuznetsov), *Babi Yar: A Document in the Form of a Novel*, trans. David Floyd (New York: Farrar, Straus, and Giroux, 1970), 91, 93, 291.

7 "Shchodennyk Niny Herasymovoï—meshkanky okupovanoho m. Kyïv. 1941–1945." Tsyfrovi kolektsiï Natsional´noho muzeiu istoriï Ukraïny u Druhii svitovii viini. 16 March 2016, https://digital.warmuseum.kiev.ua/documents/9 (accessed May 30, 2021).

8 Natan M. Meir, *Kiev, Jewish Metropolis: A History, 1859–1914* (Indiana University Press, 2010); Victoria Khiterer, *Jewish City or Inferno of Russian Israel? A History of the Jews in Kiev before February 1917* (Boston: Academic Studies Press, 2016); Serhiy Bilenky, *Imperial Urbanism in the Borderlands: Kyiv, 1800–1905* (Toronto: University of Toronto Press, 2018).

9 *Encyclopaedia Britannica Online*, s. v. "Kyiv; Evolution of the Modern City," accessed November 9, 2021, https://www.britannica.com/place/Kyiv/Evolution-of-the-modern-city

10 *History of the Jews of Kiev–From the Beginning until September 1941*, accessed November 9, 2021, https://www.yadvashem.org/education/educational-materials/learning-environment/babi-yar/historical-background2.html, (accessed November 8, 2021).

11 See, for example, Martin Dean, *Collaboration in the Holocaust: Crimes of the Local Police in Belorussia and Ukraine, 1941–1944* (New York: Macmillan Press/St. Martin's Press, 2008); Wendy Lower, *Nazi Empire-Building and the Holocaust in Ukraine* (Chapel Hill: University of North Carolina Press, 2005); *The Shoah in Ukraine: History, Testimony, Representation*, eds. Ray Brandon and Wendy Lower (Bloomington and Indianapolis: University of Indiana Press, 2009).

12 On earlier discussion of the commemoration of the events in Babyn Yar, see William Korey, "A Monument over Babi Yar?" in *The Holocaust in the Soviet Union: Studies and Sources on the Destruction of the Jews in the Nazi-occupied Territories of the USSR, 1941–45*, ed. Lucjan Dobroszycki and Jeffrey Gurock (New York: M. E. Sharpe, 1993), 61–74; Jeff Mankoff, "Babi Yar and the Struggle for Memory, 1944–2004," *Ab Imperio* 2 (2004), 393–415; E. W. Clowes, "Constructing the Memory of the Holocaust: The Ambiguous Treatment of Babii Yar in Soviet Literature," *Partial Answers: Journal of Literature and the History of Ideas* 3, no. 2 (June 2005), 153–82; Jacqueline Cherepinsky, "The Absence of the Babi Yar Massacre from Popular Memory" (Ph.D. diss., West Chester University of Pennsylvania, 2010); Aleksandr Burakovskiy, "Holocaust Remembrance in Ukraine: Memorialization of the Jewish Tragedy at Babi Yar," *Nationalities Papers* 39, no. 3 (May 2011), 371–89; Serhy Yekelchyk, *Stalin's Children: Everyday Politics in the Wake of Total War* (New York: Oxford University Press, 2014), 13–33; Jacqueline Cherepinsky, "Babi Yar" in *The Holocaust: Memories and History*, ed. Viktoriia Khiterer, Ryan Barrick, and David Misal (Newcastle upon Tyne: Cambridge Studies Publishing, 2014); Vladyslav Hrynevych and Pavlo-Robert Magochii [Paul Robert Magosci], eds. *Babyn Iar: istoriia i pam'iat´* (Kyiv: Dukh i litera, 2016); Jessica Rapson, *Topographies of Suffering: Buchenwald, Babi Yar, Lidice* (New York: Berghahn, 2017), 79–113; Norman M. Naimark, "The Many Lives of Babi Yar," *Hoover Digest* 2 (Spring 2017): 176–86.

13 Earlier mentions and discussions of Babyn Yar in Ukrainian poetry include, among others, the following publications: Richard Sheldon, "The Transformations of Babi Yar," in *Soviet Society and Culture. Essays in Honor of Vera S. Dunham*, ed. Terry L. Thompson and Richard Sheldon (Boulder and London: Westview Press, 1988); Myroslav Shkandrij, *Jews in*

Ukrainian Literature (New Haven: Yale University Press, 2009); Yohanan Petrovsky-Shtern, *Anti-Imperial Choice* (New Haven: Yale University Press, 2009); Borys Chornyi [Boris Czerny], "Literaturni svidchennia masovoho znyshchennia ievreïv u Babynomu Iaru," in *Babyn Iar: masove vbyvstvo i pam'iat´ pro n´oho. Materialy mizhnarodnoï naukovoï konferentsiï 24–25 zhovtnia 2011 r., m. Kyïv*, eds. Vitalii Nakhmanovych, Anatolii Podol´skyi, Mykhailo Tiahlyi (Kyiv: Ukr. tsentr vyvchennia istoriï Holokostu, 2012), 198–210; Boris Czerny, "Témoignages et œuvres littéraires sur le massacre de Babij Jar, 1941–1948," *Cahiers du monde russe* 53, no. 4 (2012), 513–70; Asia Kovryhina-Kreidych, "Babyn Iar: literaturni svidchennia ta pryvatni versiï," in *Babyn Yar*, eds. Vladyslav Hrynevych and Paul Robert Magosci, 169–89; Iryna Zakharchuk, "Babyn Iar v khudozhnii literaturi," in *Babyn Yar*, eds. Vladyslav Hrynevych and Paul Robert Magosci, 217–252; Liubov´ Khazan, *Saga o rytsariakh Bab´ego Iara: Il´ia Erenburg, Lev Ozerov, Pavel Antokol´skii, Viktor Nekrasov, Ada Rybachuk i Vladimir Mel´nichenko, Evgenii Evtushenko, Anatolii Kuznetsov, Naum Korzhavin i drugie* (Kyiv; Jerusalem: ILEKNIF, 2018); Alessandro Achilli, "Individual, yet Collective Voices: Polyphonic Poetic Memories in Contemporary Ukrainian Literature," *Canadian Slavonic Papers* 62, no. 1 (2020): 4–26.

14 Some Kyiv-based Russophone poets remained in the city throughout the Nazi occupation. For example, Liudmila Titova, continued to live in the city until her death. Titova's untitled poem, "Prikaz podkreplialsia ugrozoi rasstrela" (An order was enforced by the threat of a firing squad; 1941) appeared in print, for the first time, in the anthology *Ekho Bab´iego Iara* (The echo of Babyn Iar; 1991). Others left the city shortly before the Red Army recaptured it, as was the case for the poet Olga Anstei (the nom de plume of Olga Shteinberg, 1912–85). Anstei's longer

poem, "Kirillovskie iary" (Kyryliv ravines), written sometime in 1941 or 1942, was published in the West at the end of the 1940s in her debut book *Dver´ v stene* (A door in the wall; Munich, 1948). On Anstei, see Vadim Kreyd, "Ainstei, Olga Nikolaevna," in *Dictionary of Russian Women Writers*, ed. B. L. Bessonov, Marina Ledkovskaia-Astman, Charlotte Rosenthal, Mary Fleming Zirin (Greenwood Publishing Group, 1994), 33–35; and Maria Bloshteyn, "Olga Anstei: A Life in Brief," *The Postil Magazine*, November 1, 2017, https://www.thepostil.com/olga-anstei-a-life-in-brief, (accessed on April 15, 2021).

15 A. Anatolii (Kuznetsov), *Babii Iar: Roman-dokument*, 2nd edition (Munich: Posev, 1973). The 1970s editions published by German-based publishing house Posev were the first uncensored editions. By using italics and square brackets, Kuznetsov recreated in the Posev editions the officially-accepted Soviet text, as well as the censor's exclusions and the author's additions to the book as prepared in 1969. For comparison, see the original 1966 publication in the *Iunost´* journal and the 1967 edition brought out by the publishing house Molodaia Gvardiia. Another interesting work of prose about Babyn Yar is by Dokiia Humenna, a Ukrainian writer who moved westward before the Red Army recaptured Kyiv and at the end of the 1940s settled down in the United States. During the war, the author kept a diary that would later become the foundation for a novel, written between 1946 and 1949 and published in 1956. *Khreshchatyi iar (Kyiv 1941–43): Roman-khronika* (New York: Slovo, 1956) was one of the earliest—if not the very first—literary depictions of Kyiv during the war written in Ukrainian by someone with first-hand experience of the city during the Nazi occupation. For a nuanced description of Humenna's diary and its subsequent conversion into a novel, see Myroslav Shkandrij, "Dokiia Humenna's Representation

of the Second World War in Her Novel and Diary," *Harvard Ukrainian Studies* 32/33, part 2, *Zhnyva: Essays Presented in Honor of George G. Grabowicz on His Seventieth Birthday* (2011–2014), 665–79, and an adapted version of that in Myroslav Shkandrij, *Ukrainian Nationalism: Politics, Ideology, and Literature, 1929–1956*, 253–67. For analysis of the responses and readers' feedback to Humenna's novel, see Myroslav Shkandrij, "Dokia Humenna's Depiction of the Second World War and the OUN in *Khreshchatyi iar*: How Readers Responded," *East/West: Journal of Ukrainian Studies* 3, no. 1 (2016), 89–109.

16 Ilya Kukulin, "Afterword," in *Written in the Dark: Five Poets in the Siege of Leningrad*, ed. Polina Barskova (Brooklyn: Ugly Duckling Presse, 2016), 129.

17 Czesław Miłosz, *New Collected Poems, 1931–2001* (New York: Ecco Press, 2003), 63.

18 Olga Gershenson, *The Phantom Holocaust: Soviet Cinema and Jewish Catastrophe* (New Brunswick, New Jersey: Rutgers University Press, 2013), 2.

19 "Historian Timothy Snyder: Babi Yar A Tragedy for All Ukrainians," *Radio Free Europe/Radio Liberty*, September 29, 2016, https://www.rferl.org/a/ukraine-babi-yar-historian-snyder-tragedy-for-all/28022569.html (accessed May 30, 2021).

20 Iurii Ianovs′kyi, "Vatutin pid Kyievom," in *Vybrane* (Kyiv: Derzhavne vydavnytstvo khudozhn′oï literatury, 1949), 184.

21 Dovzhenko, *Shchodennykovi zapysy, 1939–1956* (Kharkiv: Folio, 2013), 299.

22 Dovzhenko, *Shchodennykovi zapysy, 1939–1956*, 265.

23 Dovzhenko, *Shchodennykovi zapysy, 1939–1956*, 301.

24 Maxim D. Shrayer, *I Saw It: Ilya Selvinsky and the Legacy of Bearing Witness to the Shoah* (Boston: Academic Studies Press, 2013), 116.

25 On the depiction of Babyn Yar in Russian poetry, see Maxim Shrayer, "Jewish-Russian Poets Bearing Witness to the Shoah,

1941–1946: Textual Evidence and Preliminary Conclusions," in *Studies in Slavic Languages and Literatures. ICCEES [International Council for Central and East European Studies] Congress Stockholm 2010 Papers and Contributions*, ed. Stefano Garzonio (Bologna: Portal on Central Eastern and Balkan Europe, 2011), 59–119; Maxim Shrayer, *I Saw It: Ilya Selvinsky and the Legacy of Bearing Witness to the Shoah* (Boston: Academic Studies Press, 2013); Maxim Shrayer, "Ilya Ehrenburg's January 1945 *Novy mir* cycle and Soviet Memory of the Shoah," in *Eastern European Jewish Literature of the 20th and 21st Centuries: Identity and Poetics*, ed. Klavdia Smola (Munich-Berlin: Die Welt der Slaven Sammelbände, Verlag Otto Sagner, 2013), 191–209; Maxim Shrayer, "Lev Ozerov as a Literary Witness to the Shoah in the Occupied Soviet Territories," in *The Holocaust: Memories and History*, eds. Victoria Khiterer, Ryan Barrick and David Misal (Newcastle upon Tyne: Cambridge Scholars Publishing, 2014), 176–187; Maxim Shrayer, "Pavel Antokolsky as a Witness to the Shoah in Ukraine and Poland," *Polin: Studies in Polish Jewry*, no. 28 (2015): 541–56. For comparative approaches to the study of poetry about Babyn Yar in Soviet Russian and Yiddish literature, see: Shay Arie Pilnik, "The Representation of Babi Yar in Soviet Russian and Yiddish Literature" (Ph.D. diss., The Jewish Theological Seminary of America, 2013); Naya Lekht, "Narratives of Return: Babii Iar and Holocaust Literature in the Soviet Union" (Ph.D. diss., University of California, Los Angeles, 2013).

26 Mykola Bazhan, "Maister zaliznoï troiandy," in *Tvory v chotyr´okh tomakh*, vol. 3, ed. N. Bazhan-Lauer (Kyiv: Dnipro, 1985), 65–66. Shul´man, most likely, was the artist Feliks Giterman. For his story of survival in Kyiv see: "Prishelets s togo sveta. Rasskaz Feliksa Zinov´evicha Gitermana," in *Neizvesnaia "Chernaia kniga". Materialy k "Chernoi knige" pod redaktsiei Vasiliia*

Grossmana i Il´i Erenburga, ed. Il´ia Al´tman (Moscow: AST; Corpus, 2015), 22–26.

27 See page **53** in this collection.

28 Peter Grose, "Boys of Kiev Play Ball on Babi Yar," *The New York Times* (June 26, 1966), L5.

29 Yohanan Petrovsky-Shtern, "A Paradigm-Changing Day: Jews, Ukrainians, and the 25th Anniversary of the Babyn Yar," a Petryshyn Memorial Lecture delivered at the Ukrainian Research Institute at Harvard University, March 10, 2021, https://www.youtube.com/watch?v=cufoXa3axiM, (accessed April 15, 2021).

30 Ivan Dziuba, "On the Twenty-Fifth Anniversary of the Murders in Baby Yar," trans. Marta Olinyk, *Polin: Studies in Polish Jewry*. Vol. 26: *Jews and Ukrainians*, ed. Yohanan Petrovsky-Shtern and Anthony Polonsky (Littman Library of Jewish Civilization, 2014), 384.

31 Grose, "Boys of Kiev Play Ball on Babi Yar," *New York Times*, L5.

32 For more information on the Jewish rally in 1942, see notes to the poem "To the Jewish people" by Maksym Ryl´s´kyi on p. **187** in this volume.

33 Lina Kostenko, *Poezii̇̈*, ed. Osyp Zinkevych (Ukraïns´ke Vydavnytstvo Smoloskyp im. V. Symonenka, 1969), 15.
The Ukrainian original:

Кажуть люди: десь тут у долині
Всі живцем закопані були.
Тут Одарка невсипуща мати,
Миротворця дитячих чвар.
Тут Лаврін, прислів'ями багатий,
І Кривенко, сивий чоботар.
Тут Юрко і чорноока Хана,
Всі малі товариші мої.
Тут земля, а в ній глибока рана,
Не чіпайте, боляче землі.

34 *Holodomor Reader: A Sourcebook on the Famine of 1932–1933 in Ukraine,* eds. Bohdan Klid and Alexander J. Motyl (Toronto: CIUS Press, 2012); *The Great West Ukrainian Prison Massacre of 1941: A Sourcebook*, eds. Ksenya Kiebuzinski and Alexander J. Motyl (Amsterdam: Amsterdam University Press, 2016); Tamara Hundorova, *The Post-Chornobyl Library: Ukrainian Postmodernism of the 1990s*, trans. Sergiy Yakovenko (Boston: Academic Studies Press, 2019). On the literary works on Chernobyl, see Maxim Tarnawsky, "The Literary Fallout of the Chornobyl," The Danylo Husar Struk Memorial Lecture at University of Toronto, May 26, 2006, http://lab.chass.utoronto.ca/rescentre/slavic/ukr/audio/StrukLectures/Tarnawsky-2006.mp3 (accessed May 30, 2021).

35 A short citation and note on each poem can be found in the annotations at the end of this volume.

36 Amir Weiner, *Making Sense of the War: The Second World War and the Fate of the Bolshevik Revolution* (Princeton: Princeton University Press, 2001), 231–32.

37 In Poland, for example, the first anthology of poems on the Holocaust was published as early as 1947. See *Pieśń ujdzie cało: antologia wierszy o żydach pod okupacją niemiecką*, ed. Michał Maksymilian Borwicz. (Warszawa: Centralna żydowska historyczna komisja w Polsce, 1947).

38 Iurii Kaplan, ed., *Ekho Bab´ego Iara: poeticheskaia antologiia* (Kyiv: Rif, 1991); Iurii Kaplan, ed., *Vidlunnia Babynoho Iaru: poetychna antolohiia*, introduction by Ivan Dziuba, 2nd ed. (Kyiv: Iuh, 2001), Iurii Kaplan, *Vidlunnia Babynoho Iaru: poetychna antolohiia*, introduction by Ivan Dziuba, preface by Oleksandr Moroz, 3rd ed. . (Kyiv: Iuh, 2006).

39 *Bol´*, ed. Ritalii Zaslavskii (Kyiv: Raduga, 1991).

40 Il´ia Levitas, ed. *Babii Iar v serdtse: poeziia* (Kyiv: Holovna spetsializovana redaktsiia literatury movamy natsional´nykh menshyn, 2001). Other Babyn Yar-related books edited by

Levitas include *Pravedniki Bab´ego Iara* (Kyiv: Evreiskii sovet Ukrainy; Fond "Pamiat´ Bab´ego Iara", 2001), *Pamiat´ Bab´ego Iara: vospominaniia, dokumenty* (Kyiv: Evreiskii sovet Ukrainy: Fond "Pamiat´ Bab´ego Iara", 2001), *Babii Iar: spasiteli i spasennye* (Kyiv: Tipografiia "Izdatel´stvo Stal´, 2005), *Babii Iar: kniga pamiati* (Kyiv: Stal´, 2005).

41 Poems in Russian were written by Russian poets and by Ukrainian Russophone poets. The Yiddish poems were not presented in their original language in the anthologies mentioned, but instead were translated into Russian. Some Russophone poems were written during or shortly after the war, as were those by Lev Ozerov and Ilya Ehrenburg (both poets, incidentally, who were originally from Kyiv). To the corpus of texts in Russian belong poems by Yevgeny Yevtushenko and Aleksandr Galich. Ukrainian Russophone poets included Iurii Kaplan, Ritalii Zaslavskii, Helii Aronov, and others. Russian- and Yiddish-language texts have—unlike Ukrainian-language texts—represented an important part of the canon of works on Babyn Yar in their respective languages. Thus, poetry about Babyn Yar in Russian and Yiddish has been a topic of interest for researchers and scholars, especially in comparative studies. While considering the editorial approaches to the compilation of those anthologies, the editors appear to have been interested in the poetry by Yiddish-language poets that were connected to Ukraine. Such poets were often born in Ukraine but moved elsewhere later, or continued to reside there, as did, for instance, Riva Baliasna, Shloima Cherniavs´kyi, Mykhailo Mohylevych, and Aron Vergelis. Lastly, it should be pointed out that anthologies, in most cases, have been dominated by poems in Russian, with poems written in Ukrainian assigned second or third place in prominence. Yet all of these volumes deserve our attention and

an understanding of the focus, availability, and accessibility of poems on Babyn Yar in the early 1990s and 2000s.

42 Quoted in Iryna Klymova, "Babyn Iar u skul´pturi ta zhyvopysi," in *Babyn Yar: Istoriia i pam'iat´*, eds. Vladyslav Hrynevych and Pavlo Robert Magochi [Paul Robert Magosci], 278.

43 D. Fedorovs´kyi, "Bab'iachyi iar (V maisterni khudozhnyka V. Ochynnikova)," *Radians´ke mystetstvo* (July 30, 1947), https://old.archives.gov.ua/Sections/Babyn_Yar/CDAMLM/index.php?28, (accessed November 11, 2021).

44 David G. Roskies and Naomi Diamant, *Holocaust Literature: A History and Guide* (Boston, Mass.: Brandeis University Press, 2012), 3.

Arkadii Anin (1925–2015) was born in Shepetivka and fought in the Soviet army during the World War II. From 1952 to 1989 he worked as a stomatologist at the Kyiv Medical Institute. In 1989, he published his first collection, *Liubit′ by i liubit′* (To never stop loving), in Russian. In 1990, he moved to Israel. He published two more collections of poetry: *Bessonnik: Stikhi raznykh let* (Dictionary of dreamlessness: Verses from various years, Bnei Brak, 1995), in Russian, and *Dotyk* (Touch; 1997), in Ukrainian.

Монолог ненародженого пам’ятника

Мене немає в кам’яному рукотворі.
І болем бронзовим я теж не кровоточу.
Лежу,
          гранітна брила,
                              тихо, без докорів,
і на дорозі —
                    від життя
                              до смерті,
усім дивлюся в очі.
Я — камінь, місце свідчення,
Я — віха.
Не треба галасу, збіговиська, промов.
Приходьте і прислухайтеся —
                                        диха
Земля людьми.
                              То дихає любов
І молить нині сущих —
                                        долюбити
Все, що живе навкруг,
                                    і — під землею...
Минуле не забудьте,
                                    майбутнє не згубіть!..—
Любіть Любов!
Ви —
          сироти
                    без неї.

[1997]

Monologue of a Monument Never Built

I'm not carved from stone.
And I don't bleed with bronze pain either.
I'm lying,
a granite block,
silently, without complaint,
and on the road
from life
to death,
I look everyone in the eyes.
I'm a rock, a place of testimony,
I'm a milestone.
No need for fuss, rallies, speeches.
Come and listen—
the earth
breathes with people.
Love breathes
and begs every living person
to love
everything that is above
and beneath the earth...
Don't forget the past,
don't lose the future!...
Cherish Love!
You're
orphans
without it.

[1997]

Монолог пам'ятника

Мені дозволено
Тут
Спати.
Я на задвірках змерз лежати.
Мене замучили по кабінетах
бездушні партапологети.
Разом із солдатом, і матросом,
і партизаном —
Весь мій рід
тут спить навічно під покосом, —
тут був тотальний геноцид!!!
Прийдіть, закохані, із квітами,
лишіть сльозу, низькій уклін —
з серцями, щирістю зігрітими.
Аби — без війн.
Аби — без війн.

[1997]

Monologue of the Monument

I'm allowed
to sleep
here.
I got cold lying in the storage yard.
I was tortured in party offices
by soulless apologists.
Together with soldier, sailor
and partisan—
All my people
sleep here forever under a layer of grass,
here was a complete genocide!
Come, lovers, with flowers,
leave a tear, take a low bow—
with hearts warmed by sincerity.
Just no more war.
Just no more war.

[1997]

Mykola Bazhan (1904–1983), one of the most important poets of the 1920s and 1930s, was born in Kam'ianets-Podilskyi. Bazhan emerged as a futurist; however, in the 1920s and early 1930s, he embraced Romantic Expressionism. During his extensive career spanning some six decades, Bazhan was prolific as a poet, literary critic, translator, editor, and political and cultural figure. His early collections of poetry include *17-i patrul´* (The seventeenth patrol; 1926), *Rizblena tin´* (The sculpted shadow; 1927), *Budivli* (Edifices; 1929), the longer poem *Sliptsi* (Blind bards; 1930–31). A four-volume edition of his work was published in the 1980s. An anthology of his early works in Ukrainian with English translations, *Quiet Spiders of the Hidden Soul*, edited by Oksana Rosenblum, Lev Fridman, and Anzhelika Khyzhnia, appeared in 2020.

Яр

Руді провалля, глинища зелені,
Завалений зотлілим сміттям рів.
Жахаючись, вривається в легені
Зловіщий вітер ржавих пустирів.

Не бліднути, не скніти не здригатись —
— Стоять, як суд! Як войовник стоять!
Замало клятв, щоб ними присягатись,
Щоб проклинати — не стає проклять.

Звичайний яр, брудний і неохайний,
Тремтляві віти двох блідих осик.
Ні, це не тиша! Незгасимий крик,
Ста тисяч серць, предсмертний крик одчайний.

Сріблястий попіл спалених кісток.
Людського лоба тріснутий шматок.

Розпались яру здвигнуті укоси.
Позвуть із ями золотисті коси —

В землі не скрилось, тліном не взялось
Витке і ніжне золото волось.
Блищать на мокрій твані крутоярів
Розбите скло старечих окулярів,

І дотліває, кинутий на бік,
Закровлений дитячий черевик.

Ravine

Auburn chasms, green clay canyons,
A ravine full of smoldering garbage.
It's terrifying, this wasteland blasts
A sinister wind through your lungs.

Don't blanch, don't wilt, don't shiver—
Stand as if you're in court! Stand like a warrior!
There aren't any oaths you can take,
You don't even have the right to expletives.

A typical ravine, dirty and shabby,
The trembling branches of two pale aspens.
No, this isn't silence! Endless howling,
A desperate death cry of one hundred thousand hearts.

Silver dust of burnt bones.
A cracked piece of human forehead.

The ravine's shifting slopes fall apart.
Golden braids crawl from the ravine—

The delicate curly golden hair
Didn't disappear underground, turn to dust.
The broken lens of an old man's glasses
Glitters in the wet mud of steep ravines,

And smoldering, thrown to the side,
A child's shoe covered in blood.

Зарито в землю, втоптано у глину
Жахливий слід стотисячного тліну;

Слизький і жирний замісився глей
Розкришеними рештками людей.

Це тут ревіли вогнища багрові,
Це тут шкварчали нафти ручаї,
І в трупах жадно рилися палії,
Шукаючи скарбів на мертвякові.

Тяжкий, гнітучий і нестерпний дим
Підносився над моторошним яром.
Він дихав смертю, він душив кошмаром,
Вповзав в доми страховищем глухим.

Багрово-чорні полохи блукали
По занімілій від жаху землі,
Кривавили злим відблиском квартали,
Бруднили житель київських шпилі.

І бачив люд з своїх скорботних сховищ,
Як за вінцем кирилівських будов,
За тополями дальніми кладовищ
Горіла страшно їхня плоть і кров.

Могильний вітер з тих ярів повіяв —
Чад смертних вогнищ, тіл димучих згар
Дивився Київ гнівнолиций Київ,
Як в полум'ї метався Бабин Яр.

Buried in soil, trampled in clay,
Horrific signs, the traces of one hundred thousand;

The soil grows slippery, viscous, and changes
Color from mixing with human remains.

Here is where the crimson fire roared,
Here is where the streams of gasoline sizzled,
And those in charge of burning first greedily
Ransacked the corpses for loot.

Thick, deplorable, unbearable smoke
Rose high above the hideous ravine.
It exhaled death, choked people with terror,
Ravaged houses like a poltergeist.

Scarlet and black terrors wandered
Across the land numb from horror,
Oozed through neighborhoods covering all
In blood, reflecting evil, soiling Kyiv's spires.

And people saw from their mournful shelters
How beyond the crowns of Kyryliv's buildings,
Beyond the poplars of distant cemeteries,
Their flesh and blood were brutally burned.

Sepulchral wind blew from those ravines—
The smoke of deadly fires, of burning bodies.
Kyiv watched, Kyiv with its irate face,
While flames rampaged through Babyn Yar.

За пломінь цей не може буть покути,
За погар цей нема ще міри мсти.
Будь проклят той, хто звабиться забути!
Будь проклят той, хто скаже нам — «прости» !

1943

For this flame there can't be any atonement,
For this scorched terrain there's no measure of vengeance.
Be damned, anyone tempted to forget!
Be damned, anyone who tells us to forgive.

1943

Valeriia Bohuslavs′ka (b. 1939) is a poet and translator. She began writing in Russian but later switched to writing and publishing poetry and translations in Ukrainian. Since 1998, Bohuslavs′ka has published more than six collections of poetry. She has also translated work from Russian, English and Yiddish. She is the coeditor, with Velvl Chernin, of *Antolohiia ievreis′koï poezii* (An anthology of Jewish poetry; 2007), a volume of poetry in Yiddish translated into Ukrainian.

Маріанні Кіяновській — на книжку «Бабин Яр. Голосами»

Кривавим лепом глини рот забито,
Пробилось тільки спрагле слово:
«Мушу!»
...З кометно-коматозної орбіти
Душа постукала поетці в душу.

Крізь Бабин Яр, крізь Куренівські селі
Вона прибилась, мовби до оселі
Своєї — ніби серце стисла в жмені,
Неначе мовила: скажи за мене,
Вгадай моє сплюндроване імення,
Ні — якщо можеш, перевтілься в мене!

І ти вже Маріам, не Маріанна,
Роз'ятрену свою смертельну рану
Несеш у Бабин Яр, на місце страти —
За всіх, кому заступниця й сестра ти.

2018

For Marianna Kiyanovska—in Response to Her Book *The Voices of Babyn Yar*

Mouth stuffed with bloody clay,
Only thirsty words broke through:
"I must!"
... From the comet's sleepy orbit
A voice rapped on the poet's soul.

Through Babyn Yar, through the Kureniv villages,
She made her way as though coming home,
As if she clenched her soul in her fist,
As if she'd come to say: speak for me,
Guess my decimated name,
No—if you can, embody me!

And now you've become Miriam, not Marianna,
You carry your aching deadly wound
To Babyn Yar, to the place of execution—
For all whose guardian and sister you've become.

2018

Leonid Cherevatenko (1938–2014) was a poet, screenwriter, and literary critic. Born in Dnipropetrovsk (now, Dnipro), he graduated from the Taras Shevchenko Kyiv National University and the Higher Screenwriting Courses at the Goskino USSR (State Committee for Cinematography USSR) in Moscow. During his lifetime he authored four collections of poetry, wrote screenplays for a dozen feature and documentary films, edited and compiled books, and translated poetry. He is also known for his articles in the field of film studies. A recipient of the Taras Shevchenko Prize in Cinematography, he died in Kyiv.

Мікеланджело

ось аматорське фото:
із архівів фашизму:

глинистою лощовиною
тече повільна ріка
блідих переплетених тіл
пекельне видиво Мікеланджело
голі женщини
голі діти
голі каліки й діди
всіх їх забито в потилицю

а поміж них мужчини
намитні-валуни серед поля
голі горбасті руки свої
поміж калік та дітей
хоронять
і схоронити не можуть
роздягнені догола
мужчини
їх так само забито в потилицю

ненавидне видиво Мікеланджело

Бабин Яр. 1966

Michelangelo

here's an amateur photo
from the archives of fascism:

through a rotten ravine
flows a slow river
of pallid intertwined bodies
a hateful scene from Michelangelo
naked women
naked children
naked disabled and old men
they all are shot in the neck

and among them men
like boulders in the middle of the field
their naked gnarled hands
among the disabled and children
they bury
and can't bury
men totally
naked
who were also shot in the neck

a hateful scene from Michelangelo

Babyn Yar, 1966

Медуза Горгона

То ви гадаєте, зондеркоманда,
Що працювала в Бабинім Яру,
Складалася з хвостатих і рогатих
Страховищ — з новочасних квазімодо?

Були це браві, жваві, терті хлопці,
До випивки охочі й закусону
І ласі до жіноцтва. Тож не дивно,
Що закортіло їм пожартувати:
На виступ над безоднею вони
Коляску викотили зі старою
Жидівкою, аби помилувалась
Хоч перед смертю, як іде в правічність
Народ її, що тяжко завинив
Перед людьми і Господом. Лунали
З тієї прірви лемент і волання,
Безладна крикнява, гурчання кулеметів
І стогони цнотливих, непочатих
Дівчаток: їх убивці ґвалтували
У матерів нестямних і старої
Перед очима.

Сторчма у неї коси піднялись:
Вона тепер нагадувала третю
З горгон — Медузу. Смертну.
Тільки не знайшовся
Герой Персей, що їй би відрубав
Обвиту гаддям голову. Їй також
Не пощастило в камінь обернути
Все те, що бачила. Тож пустуни

The Gorgon Medusa

So, do you really think the death squads
Working Babyn Yar were full
Of monsters with horns and tails,
A bunch of modern Quasimodos?

They were brave, energetic, experienced guys,
They loved their food and drink—
And especially their women. It's no wonder
They wanted to mess around:
They rolled an old Jewish woman
In a wheelchair to the edge of the ravine
So before dying she could admire
The way her people were entering eternity,
Guilty before man and God. Lamentations
Came from down below, chaotic shouting,
The roar of machine guns, the groans
Of virgin, untouched girls: the killers
Raped them in front of their grief-mad
Mothers and the old woman.

Her braids stood up straight:
Now she looked like the third
Among the gorgons—Medusa. The mortal one.
Perseus, the hero who could have
Chopped off her snake-covered head,
Wasn't around. But she wasn't lucky enough
To turn all that she saw to stone.

Розважились, набавились. Надвечір,
Коли кінчався їхній день робочий,
Із реготом і свистом закотили
Стару жидівку, в котрої від жаху
Волосся дибилось на голові,
Туди — в безодняву, в провалля,
в безвість.

2010

Those pranksters just kept carousing.
That evening, their workday done,
Roaring with laughter and whistling,
They rolled the old Jewish woman, whose
Hair rose up from terror, and pushed her
Off—into the abyss, into the gorge,
                                        into obscurity.

2010

Єврейське питання: рік 1941-й

Жив собі чоловік Сашка,
Була у нього сіра серм'яжка,
На голові шапочка,
А на сраці латочка…

Ось якими примовками розважав
Дітлахів сусідських, а заодно й дорослих,
Данило Іванович, дід мій любий,
За фахом електрик, який, аби трохи
Підзаробити, заходився крутити гешефти
Удвох зі своїм квартирантом Чепурняком
(Займався тобто, як нині сказали б,
Малоприбутковим бізнесом). І завжди
Чомусь виходило так, що дід позичав,
У борг давав колезі Чепурнякові,
Але ніколи копійки не заробив, навпаки —
Залишався ніби ще й винний.
Чепурнякові ж
Неначе хто шепотів на вухо
Зміни курсу: брав за старим,
Повертав за новим. І от цікаво:
Дід аніскільки не дратувався:
«Що ти хочеш? Золота голова у хлопця,
Єврейська! Ну, а я — баран з баранів!
У мене й мізки не тудою стоять…» А втім,
Яке то значення має
Після того, що сталося потім?

1941: The Jewish Question

Let me tell you about Sashka.
He wore heavy grey overalls,
On his head, a hat,
On his butt, a patch…

With these ditties my beloved grandfather,
Danylo Ivanovych, an electrician by profession,
Entertained neighborhood children,
And, at the same time, adults. In order to earn
Extra money, he began a side-hustle
With his tenant Chepurniak. Somehow
It always turned out that grandpa would lend
Money to his partner Chepurniak,
But he never got a penny back. On the contrary,
He always owed more.
It was
As if someone whispered in Chepurniak's ear
Change the rate: he would borrow by one,
And return by another. And what's
Interesting: grandfather was never annoyed:
"What do you want? The guy has a brilliant mind,
A Jewish one! And I'm a ram among rams!
My head doesn't work that way…" Anyway,
Does it really matter
After what happened later?

А потому приперлися фашисти.
Знов-таки —
Серед найперших про це довідався Чепурняк:
Не приблизно, а точно він знав, що німці вступлять,
Що необхідно тікати, бігти звідси.
Лахи свої поскидавши у торби,
Невідомо як добув вантажівку
Та й подався з усім сімейством на схід.

Зосталася тільки найстарша дочка
З ім'ям біблійним Єва,
Бо мала підлітка-сина Яшку,
Що звався по-вуличному Лазько.
Покручені, наче в комахи, руки і ноги
Не дозволяли йому нормально
Пересуватись. Катали його у візочку,
І то була неабияка втіха для всієї малечі,
Для отої дрібної босоти. Урвителі,
Гасали ми з безпорадним Лазьком,
Бешкетували, дуріли. І він дурів і радів
З нами разом і реготав безтурботно.

(Мабуть, з цього й варто було
Розпочинати оповідь, та вже так вийшло,
Так воно склалося…)

День був сонячний, вересневий, тепленький.
Кількоро нас, дітлахів, бавилося на подвір'ї:
Галасували, тягали візочка з Лазьком,
Коли нагодився німець — один, як палець,
Молодий, симпатичний такий, білявий,
Під погоном пілотка, насвистував

Because then the Nazis showed up.
                                        Again—
Chepurniak was among the first to find out:
He wasn't guessing, he knew the Germans were coming,
That he'd better flee, run away from here.
Having packed some old clothes into bags,
He somehow managed to get a truck
And went eastward with the whole family.

Only the eldest daughter remained,
With the Biblical name of Eva,
Because she had a teenage son Yasha,
Who was called Lazko on the street.
Twisted, like insects, his arms and legs
Didn't allow him to get around
Normally. We rolled him in a wheelchair,
And it was a great joy for all kids,
Especially the little poor ones. Troublemakers,
We raced around with helpless Lazko,
We misbehaved, goofed off. And he was happy
And laughed carelessly with us.

(It's likely I should have started this story
Here, but I've already been going on,
This is how it turned out...)

It was a September day, sunny and warm.
Several of us children played in the yard:
We were loud, dragging the wheelchair with Lazko,
When a German appeared—alone, like a finger,
Young, handsome, blond,
A hat snapped to his shoulder, he whistled

Щось незнайоме. Та миттю мами
Розхапали своїх безштаньків,
Немов курчат від шуліки,
Поховали по закапелках.
Але німець одним переймався: юди?
І з'ясувавши, що юд у наявності двоє,
Подався геть. Отож на коротку часинку
Запанувала тиша. Прогримкотіла підвода.
(Річ відома: брудну роботу арійці пере-
доручали кадрам місцевим).
«Де ваші юди, показуйте!» — запитав візник сердито,
Не вистрибуючи на землю. І вийшла Єва,
З перепудженим сином викотила візочка.
Яшка-Лазько німував. Мовчало безлюдне подвір'я.
Несподівано сварка зчинилась: лементував візник:
«Я не биндюжник вам, не вантажник!
Моє діло завезти, куди накажуть,
А вантажити — не наймався!» Жіноцтво
Наше так само одговорилось. Знадвору
Хтось радив: «Гукніть поліцая». І той

Прискочив, гвинтівку приставив до клена
І з Євою вдвох висадили вони візочка
З інвалідом Лазьком на підводу.
І найстрашніше настало — прощання.

Єва спитала дозволу в поліцая,
Чи можна з сусідами попрощатись?
Нової влади прислужник знехотя буркнув:
«Про мене...»

Something unfamiliar. And instantly all the mothers
Grabbed their poor kids
Like chickens from a hawk
And hid them in corners.
But the German was concerned with one thing: Jude?
And having found out that there were two Juden,
He left. So silence settled for
A short hour. Then the carriage rattled.
(It's a known fact: the dirty work the Aryans
Entrusted to the locals.)
"Where are your Jews, show me!"
          the coachman asked angrily,
Without getting off the cart. And Eva came out,
Rolling the wheelchair with her petrified son.
Yashka-Lazko remained mute.
          The deserted courtyard silent.
Suddenly, a quarrel erupted: the coachman complained:
"I'm not a mover, I'm not a moving-man!
My job is to drive things where I'm told,
But I don't intend to load!" Our women
Also wouldn't help out. Someone in the courtyard
Advised: "Call a policeman." And one came

Quickly, put his rifle by the maple tree
And together with Eva loaded the wheelchair
With the disabled Lazko onto the carriage.
And the worst thing began, farewell.

Eva asked the policeman,
Can I say goodbye to my neighbors?
The servant of new power reluctantly muttered:
                    "Go ahead..."

Прощалася Єва, не вступаючи в хату.
«Не поминайте лихом, сусідко, — Єва мовила
Крізь вікно моїй мамі. — Непогано жили ми,
Чим могли, помагали,
Нехай, сусідко, таланить вам, а нам...» —
Показала рукою в небо.
І поки
Не обійшла усіх, поліцай понуро
Дивився кудись набік...

Прогримкотіла востаннє підвода
По старій, ще з царських часів, бруківці.
Більше ніхто не бачив
Ані Єви, ні Яшки-Лазька.
Сторонні люди казали: євреїв
Постріляли за містом, у степу й закопали
У протитанковому рову, який проте
Фашистів не зупинив.
Старий Чепурняк
Повернувся додому з евакуації.
Надалі
Данило Іванович, дід мій Любий,
Дружби з ним не водив. Не зміг
Простити: покинув дочку з онуком
«Фактичеськи на погибель».
На голові шапочка,
А на сраці латочка.
Чи гарна моя казочка?

2011

Eva was saying goodbye without entering houses.
"Don't remember me poorly, neighbor," Eva told
My mother through a window. "We didn't quarrel,
We helped each other in whatever way we could,
May you have luck, my neighbor, and we..."
And she pointed to the sky.
                                        And while
She visited everyone, the policeman gloomily
Looked the other way...

The carriage rattled for the last time
On the old cobblestones from imperial days.
Nobody ever saw
Either Eva or Yashka-Lazko again.
Strangers told us: the Jews
Were shot outside the city, on the steppe, and buried
In the anti-tank trench which had failed
To stop the fascists.
                                    Old Chepurniak
Returned from evacuation after the war.
Danylo Ivanovych, my beloved grandfather,
Was no longer friends with him. He couldn't
Forgive: he left his daughter and grandson
To die.
            On his head, a hat.
            On his butt, a patch.
            Isn't my fairytale beautiful?

2011

Borys Dabo-Nikolaiev (1943–2022) is a poet, essayist and literary critic. He graduated from Taras Shevchenko University of Kyiv. During the Soviet era, he was repressed for his connections with the so-called Ukrainian bourgeois nationalists and was banned from defending his dissertation and teaching at universities. He is currently teaching Ukrainian literature at Kyiv National Linguistic University.

Випробування трагедією

шлях шлях шлях
шелех шелест
шерех
підошв
з Галицької площі
на Захід
до Сонця
антрацит наче
у Яр
Бабин
шлях
шелех шелест
шерех шерех шерех

Київ мов-чав
-чав
-чав
А чи чув
чув
чув?

2001

Tested by Tragedy

street street street
swish shoosh
swoosh of
shoe-bottoms
from Halytska square
westward
to the Sun
like anthracite
to Babyn
Yar
street
swish shoosh
swoosh swoosh swoosh

Kyiv was shh
shh
silent
But did it listen
listen
listen?

2001

Ivan Drach (1936–2018) was a poet, literary critic, translator, screenwriter, and political leader. An author of many critically acclaimed collections of poetry, nonfiction, and screenplays, in the 1980s he emerged as a political activist. He is best known for his collections *Soniashnyk* (Sunflower; 1960), *Protuberantsi sertsia* (Solar prominences of the heart; 1965), *Balady budniv* (Workday ballads; 1967), *Poezii̇̈* (Poems; 1967), and *Kyïvs´ke nebo* (Kyiv sky; 1976). A collection of his selected poetry, edited by Stanley Kunitz, appeared in English translation in 1978 under the title *Orchard Lamps*. A collection of poems about his experience in the United States, *Amerykans´kyi zoshyt* (American notebook), was published in 1980. Drach was awarded the highest literary awards in Soviet and post-Soviet Ukraine.

[22 червня 1966 року о 5 годині вечора...]

22 червня 1966 року о 5 годині вечора
Проїздили ми над Бабиним Яром
Вечірнє сонце гусло в сонній хмарі
Дядьки в кущах лежали й пили пиво
Обсмоктуючи з прицмоком тараню
Пообіч негр розлігся на колінах
Блондинистої юної красуні
Ходила сива баба і напитувала
Чи в них немає хрестиків на продаж.
Хирляві клени жухли од спекоти
І син мій спав у мене на колінах
І снився йому дикий кінь у травах
Десь гупали копри об твердь земну
Та хтось лопатами скидав на мене небо
Тверде з корінням хмар
з камінням сонця
Аж металеві кобри лампіонів
В гущавині ховали довгі шиї
І затуляв я інстинктивно сина
22 червня 1966 року о 5 годині вечора
Коли ми приїздили над Бабиним Яром

1966

[On June 22, 1966, at five in the afternoon]

On June 22, 1966, at five in the afternoon
we drove by Babyn Yar
the evening sun thickened in a sleepy cloud
men rested among the bushes and sipped beer
smacked their lips over stockfish
nearby a black man sprawled on the lap
of a young blond beauty
a silver-haired woman walked around
and asked if they were selling small crosses.
Frail maple trees withered in the heat
and my son slept on my lap
and he dreamt of a wild horse in the weeds
somewhere pile drivers pounded firm ground
and someone shoveled sky over me
firm with the roots of clouds
                                        with stones of sun
so that the metal cobras of lanterns
hid their long necks in brushwood
and I instinctively shielded my son
on June 22, 1966, at five in the afternoon
when we drove by Babyn Yar

1966

Київська легенда

Сьогодні наш шлях — через Дніпро.
Погляньте на берег, що перед вами.
Там Київ, українська земля, там діти
і дружини, батьки і матері, брати і
сестри. Вони чекають на ВАС!..
Із звернення військової ради
1-го українського фронту

— Чому ти там, діду, стоїш над Дніпром?
Чого ти там, діду, махаєш веслом?

— Стою, бо чекаю на ваші полки.
Я — Кий-перевізник з цієї ріки.

Дідусю, стривай, кулі сиплять, як град.
Дідусю, лягай, бо накриє снаряд.

— Кінчай теревені, сідай у човни.
Смолою століть просмолились вони.

Од Лаври б'є німець з гарматних пащек.
На острів Козачий пливи мені, Щек.

Ти ж, брате Хориве, прямуй на прорив. —
На весла століть налягає Хорив.

— А хто там на кручі стоїть, як мана?
Ще й руки заломлює, самотина?

A Kyiv Legend

Today our path goes across the Dnipro.
Look at the shore in front of you.
There's Kyiv, Ukrainian land, children
and wives, fathers and mothers, brothers and
sisters. They are waiting for YOU!

From the appeal of the military council of
The First Ukrainian Front

—Why are you standing above the Dnipro, grandfather?
Why, grandfather, are you waving an oar?

—I'm here because I'm waiting for our regiments.
I'm Kyi, a porter working this river.

Grandpa, wait, the bullets are raining like hail.
Grandpa, lie down, a shell might hit you.

—Stop jabbering, and get in the boat.
It's covered with the tar of centuries.

Near the Lavra a German opens cannon-jaws.
Sail to the Cossack island, Shchek.

You, brother Khoryv, break through.
Khoryv plunges the oars of centuries.

—And who's standing on the cliff like a ghost,
Wringing her hands in sorrow? You, loneliness?

— То Либідь-сестриця, закута в дротах,
Шугає тевтонський над Либіддю птах.

— А що то за дивні-предивні тони?
— Повішені дзвонять, мов київські дзвони!

Заложників тисячі там, на Подолі,
Замучених, гнаних, без хліба і солі.

— А що там клекоче крізь погар-пожар?
— Начинений людом лихий Бабин яр.

— А там ген тріпоче вогненний намет?
— Там стогне підпалений університет!

— Які ж бо дими Київ наш облягли...
— Як пекла два роки — то скільки ж золи?

Вогненний завис понад рікою шквал.
До Кия старого іде генерал,
А Кий йому в каску води набира —
Ватутін п'є воду священну з Дніпра...

1976

—This is Lybid′, our sister, wrapped in barbed wire,
A Teutonic bird rustling above her.

—And what are those strange tones?
—The hanged ones ring like Kyiv bells!

There are thousands of hostages there, in Podil,
Tortured, persecuted, without bread and salt.

—And what is gurgling through the fire?
—Evil Babyn Yar, filled with people.

—And over there, is that a tent on fire?
—There groans the burning university!

—What fires besieged our Kyiv...
—If two years of hell, then how much ash?

A burst of flame is hanging over the river.
An old general goes to old Kyi.
And Kyi gets him water in a helmet—
Vatutin drinks holy water from the Dnipro.

1976

Hryhorii Fal′kovych (b. 1940) is a poet, a children's poet, and director of the Sholem Aleichem Jewish Cultural Educational Fellowship. He studied at the Taras Shevchenko Kyiv State University and later worked at the Oleksandr Potebnia Institute of Linguistics. Fal′kovych has authored more than a dozen poetry collections as well as children's books. His works appear in Russian, English, Yiddish, and Hebrew translation. He lives and works in Kyiv.

[Із тої страшної святої пори]

Із тої страшної святої пори
Я не забуду ніколи:
По Бабинім Ярі гонили вітри
Перекотиполе.

Сконали кістки, роздоріжжя, слова,
Чи, може, здалося,
Котилася світом не сива трава —
Волосся. Волосся…

На мить притамує. І знов кружеля.
І знову — дорога.
Його з-під землі відпустила земля,
Не знаю, для чого.

Перекотиполе, перекотиполе,
Пам’ять мою відпусти.
Через мої болі, їх і так доволі,
Перекоти, перекоти.

Ми геть усі твоя паства
Поміж справ і думок.
Он вже й сонячне пасмо
Береться в клубок.

Перекотиполе, перекотиполе,
Душу мою відпусти.
Через мої болі,
Через мої долі,
Перекоти.
Перекоти.

1989–90

[From that horrible holy time]

From that horrible holy time
I will never forget:
The wind blew tumbleweeds
Across Babyn Yar.

Bones, crossroads, words, all faded away,
Or maybe it just seemed so to me.
But the wind rolled hair, not gray grass,
Across the world. Hair...

It stops for a second. And it rolls again.
And again—down the road.
The earth sent it forth from underground,
I have no idea why.

Tumbleweed, tumbleweed,
Leave my memory alone.
Past my pain, I've had enough,
Roll me over, roll me over.

We're all your congregation
Despite our thoughts and deeds.
See the sun's threads
Tighten into a knot.

Tumbleweed, tumbleweed,
Leave my soul alone.
Past my pain,
Past my fate,
Roll me over,
Roll me over.

1989–90

[Бабине літо по Бабинім Ярі]

Бабине літо по Бабинім Ярі
Разом із осінню ходить у парі:
Ходить, шукає бабине літо
Нашу рідню, що в тім ярі убито…

Бабиним Яром блукає і досі
Бабине літо — київська осінь.

1989–90

[Indian summer in Babyn Yar]

Indian summer in Babyn Yar
Walks hand in hand with the fall:
Indian summer walks, looking for
Our relatives killed in that ravine...

Across Babyn Yar, Indian Summer
Still wanders—a Kyiv fall.

1989–90

[Переддень священної суботи]

Переддень священної суботи
Стишує хронологічний лік.
На кордоні нашої скорботи
Зупинився сорок перший рік.

Всесвіте, чи Космосе, чи Боже —
Той, що все скеровує звідтіль!
Та невже ніхто нам не поможе
Не забути — втамувати біль?

Хай не все простити — відпустити
Від душі зненависть, мсту і гнів,
Щоб могли збагнуть хоч наші діти
Вищий смисл тих вересневих днів.

Всі ми вийшли з Бабиного Яру.
Страшно повертатися туди,
Боже! Оджени мару і хмару,
На землі нас більше не суди…

1989–90

[On the eve of the holy Sabbath]

On the eve of the holy Sabbath
The measure of time slows down.
On the border of our sorrow
The year forty-one rests.

The Universe, or the Cosmos, or God—
The one who directs from out there!
Is anyone going to help us not to
Forget but at least to soothe the pain?

If not forgive everything, then let go
Hatred, vengeance, and rage from the soul.
So that at least our children can understand
The deeper meaning of those September days.

We all came out of Babyn Yar.
It's frightening to go back there, God!
Chase away specters and clouds
And don't judge us on earth...

1989–90

Moisei Fishbein (1946–2020) was an award-winning Ukrainian-Jewish poet, essayist, and translator. An author of seven collections of poems, one collection of children's poetry, and translations from many languages including German, Yiddish, Hebrew, French, Polish, and Russian, he was a recipient of the Vasyl′ Stus Prize and a member of the Ukrainian Center of the International PEN Club and the National Union of Writers of Ukraine. In 1978, Fishbein immigrated to Israel. He later took a job as a correspondent for Radio Liberty/Radio Free Europe in Munich, Germany, before returning to Ukraine in 2003.

Яр

I

У вранішню тишу
б́ються крила птахів.
… Самотній голос.
Самотня зірка.
Ще не зітерті
вчорашні сліди,
вечір без колискової.
Ще з люстра не зникли
вчорашні обличчя.
Ще спить
Рохеле без дірки в скроні.
Самотній голос.
Вже зірки нема.
Птахи дивляться на землю
з холодного неба.
Човгання. Гамір. Рипіння. Тупіт.
Вони йдуть
холодною твердою бруківкою,
тисячі люду
йдуть між твердих невблаганних стін,
вони несуть
Рохеле без дірки в скроні,
ось вона, скроня,
дитяча скроня без дірки,
вони несуть її туди, до кулеметів.
Човгання. Тупіт. Рипіння. Гамір.
З неба
на землю
дивляться птахи.

Ravine

I

Into the morning silence
the bird wings beat.
A solitary voice.
A solitary star.
Yesterday's traces
aren't erased yet,
an evening without a lullaby.
Rokhele still sleeps
with no hole in her temple.
A solitary voice.
The star is already gone.
Birds observe the ground
from a cold sky.
Scuffle. Clatter. Squeak. Tramp.
They walk
on cold firm cobblestones,
they carry
Rokhele with no hole in her temple,
here it is, her temple,
a child's temple with no hole,
they carry her there, to the machine-guns.
Scuffle. Clatter. Squeak. Tramp.
From the sky
the birds observe
the ground.

II

Понад Бабиним Яром летять журавлі —
вересневе ридання.
Понад Бабиним Яром летять журавлі —
як надія остання.
Чорні тіні летять у важкій тишині,
у своїй самотині,
понад осінь летять, понад ночі і дні
ці тіла журавлині.
І несуть недосяжність на кожнім крилі,
і зникають у мреві.
Понад Бабиним Яром летять журавлі,
ці плачі вересневі.

1974 рік, Київ

II

Above Babyn Yar the cranes fly—
the wailing of September.
Above Babyn Yar the cranes fly—
like the last hope.
The black shadows fly in a dark silence,
in their solitude.
Above the fall they fly, above nights and days
these bodies of cranes.
And they carry the unattainable on each wing
and disappear into a mirage.
Above Babyn Yar the cranes fly—
these lamentations of September.

1974, Kyiv

Iakiv Hal′perin (also known as Iakiv Halych and Mykola Pervach; 1921–43) was a poet and author who wrote in Ukrainian and Russian. Before the war, he published in *Literaturna hazeta* and during the war he received a fake identification card that enabled him to publish his writings in *Ukraïns′ke slovo, Lytavry* and *Proboiem* (Prague). Posthumously, his poems were anthologized in the book *Piatnadtsat′ poetov — piatnadtsat′ sudeb* (Fifteen poets, fifteen fates; 2001), *Sto russkikh poetov o Kieve* (One hundred Russian poets on Kyiv; 2001), *Sto poetov o liubvi* (One hundred poets on love; 2001). He was arrested and executed by the Nazis in 1943.

Сміх

Ви чули —
Весіння злива пройшла,
шпурляючи град і грім?
Поетам снились солодкі сни
та безліч блискавих рим,
Їм бачилось: рима на риму йшла,
оди строчились вшквар —
У видавництві чемний касир
сплачував гонорар.
Але ж не стрінути Музи їм,
не бачити Музи їм —
Вона співуча та навісна,
і дасться лише навісним.
Я цілував її губи п'янкі
та на руках ніс.
Осінь ішла, хуга ішла —
зорі падали вниз.
Я говорив їй: будь-що-будь —
з тобою життя пройду:
Бачу біду, чую біду,
передчуваю біду!
Але залізо в жилах моїх,
пломінь в очах моїх,
А на вустах — тонких і злих —
непереборний сміх.
О, не забути мені, не забуть
синіх осінніх днів.
Стали жорсткими очі мої,
в серці моєму гнів.

Laughter

Did you hear the spring
downpour passing
bringing hail and thunder?
The poets had sweet dreams
full of flashing rhymes,
They saw rhyme fighting rhyme,
their odes hastily written—
In the publishing house a diligent
accountant paying an advance.
They won't encounter the Muse,
they won't see her—
She sings and is powerful—
but only the mighty ones will hear her.
I kissed her drunken mouth
and carried her in my arms.
Autumn coming, snowstorm coming,
the stars falling down.
I told her: whatever happens—
I'll walk through life with you:
I see trouble, I hear trouble,
I sense trouble!
But the steel in my veins,
flame in my eyes,
And on my lips—thin and evil—
irresistible laughter.
O, I won't forget, won't forget
those blue fall days.
My eyes grew cruel,
anger in my heart.

Застерігає Коханка мене:
    «Плач, скаженій, а пиши!»
«Де ти?» — питають я у душі —
    і не знаходжу душі.
Але відрізує Гнів: «я тут!»
    ненависть каже: «є!».
— Бери тріпочаче горе це —
    воно по праву твоє!
Ні, не шукатиму вороття,
    ні, не знайду каяття —
Болями, радощами, слізьми
    приймаю тебе, Життя!
Болями, радощами, слізьми,
    останнім тхнінням клянусь:
Я ще, людоньки, посміюсь,
    люто ще посміюсь!

1941

My Mistress warns me:
  "Cry, get mad, but write!"
"Where are you," I ask my soul—
  and can't find it.
But Anger breaks in: "I'm here!"
  Hatred says, "Here I am."
—Take this trembling grief,
  it belongs to you by right!
No, I won't look for a way back,
  no, I won't look for repentance—
I accept you, Life,
  with pain, joy, and tears!
With pain, joy, and tears
  I swear by my last breath:
People, I'm going to laugh in the end,
  I'm going to laugh fiercely!

1941

Sava Holovanivs′kyi (1910–89) was a poet, fiction writer, playwright, and translator. His first collection of poetry appeared in 1927. During World War II, he was a war correspondent for the newspapers *Krasnaia zvezda* and *Za chest′ Batkivshchyny*. During his lifetime, he published over forty books of poetry, prose, translations, and plays. His collected works, in three volumes, appeared in 1981.

Вулиця Мельника

На вулиці, що йде повз Бабин Яр,
кладуть асфальт.
                    В повільній круговерті
кипить смола,
                    і роздимають жар
робітники замурзані й уперті.

Віднині й присно внаслідок старань
батьків цього уславленого міста
проляже тут без ям або ковбань,
дорога стріловидна й урочиста.

Адже не віз чи древній тарантас
тут нині їздить поспіхом мушиним,
— у вік ракет і міжпланетних трас
потрібно мчати — людям і машинам.

Ну що ж, гаразд.
                        Подяка і хвала
всім за старання пильне і велике,
хто дбає вчасно і не спроквола
про дефіцитні шини й черевики.

Шкода лише, що той, хто тут пройшов
колись на смерть у натовпі німому,
збивав об груддя шкіру підошов,
і спотикався в розпачі на ньому…

Melnyk Street

On the road that goes past Babyn Yar,
they're laying asphalt.
                    In the slow feverish whirl
tar boils, and the workers,
dirty and stubborn,
                    spread it out.

From now on, thanks to the efforts
of this celebrated city's council,
here will lie, without potholes or pits,
a road, arrow-like and solemn.

Because it's not a cart or ancient tarantass
that cruises by with the haste of ants these days—
in the age of rockets and interplanetary routes
people and cars have to rush.

Well, fine.
                Give thanks and praise
to everyone for their grand attentive efforts
to save from ruin the tires and shoes we lack,
and in such a rushed and hurried fashion.

Only it's a pity that those who were marched
in muted crowds toward their death here
had to wear down their own shoe-bottoms
as they trod along the pockmarked road in despair.

Можливо, легше біль було б терпіть
йому, ті кроки роблячи останні,
якби могильним сном заздалегідь
не дихали ці ями та ковбані.

О, краще блиск асфальтових покрить
ровів не затуляв би та вибоїв
— не тамував того, що ще болить,
і ран на скорбній вулиці не гоїв!

Нехай би йшли тим шляхом молоді
і спотикались іноді в баюрах,
щоб не забути жах, яким тоді
жили колони смертників похмурих!

...Я сам люблю цю вулицю нову,
каштанами засіяну під осінь,
у скверах свіжоскошену траву,
красу тополь і вишуканість сосон.

Та раптом давня вигулькне стіна,
і жадібно читаєш, як на шпальті,
на ній оті трагічні письмена,
яких не прочитаєш на асфальті...

1975

Maybe it would have been easier to endure
the pain while taking those last steps
if those potholes and pits couldn't breathe
their grave-like dreams in advance.

O, it'd be better if the sparkling asphalt
didn't cover the potholes and pits—
didn't curb what's still aching
and didn't heal wounds on this mournful street!

Let the young people walk along here
and sometimes trip over potholes
lest they forget the terror of those times,
th115e columns of the condemned and despairing!

...I myself love this new street,
with its crop of chestnuts in the fall,
the just-mown grass in the parks,
the beauty of poplars and elegance of pines.

But all of a sudden, an old wall will emerge,
and you read it greedily, like a newspaper page,
its tragic script, explicit captions,
which you won't read on the asphalt...

1975

Denys Holubyts´kyi (b. 1977) is a poet who writes in Russian and Ukrainian. He graduated from the Kyiv Polytechnic Institute as an engineer. Holubyts´kyi has authored three collections of poetry and recorded three musical albums. Holubyts´kyi lives and works in Kyiv, where he was born.

[Каміння моїх братів і небо моїх сестер]

Каміння моїх братів і небо моїх сестер,
тремтіння прізвищ, літер танок перед Вітом.
На вулиці ангелів мешкає бабуся. Мабуть, Естер...
Цей вересень збожеволів —
        він згарищем пахне і... квітами.
Запізно, запізно, Естер, вступатися за народ!
...Сполоханий вулик вулиці розсипався вмить.
Була і є Лютеранською стьожка на тілі міста,
шов на тлі неминучості.
Поволі вгадую тінь німецького колоніста.
Німецького?! І німію від збігу лячного.
А вулиця знову збігає в обійми Хрещатика,
        хресний торуючи шлях.
На цій найкоротшій найдовшій дорозі
не можна нічого тепер розрізнити,
        хіба тільки хлібню на розі.
А я і досі не знаю, куди мені очі діти —
сховався в мушлі не-участі.
Бабусю, бабусю, вступися!
Усі, хто там — твої діти...
Не можна летіти, вулице, не можна летіти,
потрібно спинити той каменеспад,
        часоспад, болеспад.
Повзи, Лютеранська, повзи!
Ти — вулиця люті, ти — вулиця рани смертельної.

[The stones of my brothers and the sky of my sisters]

The stones of my brothers and the sky of my sisters,
the trembling of last names,
    a dance of letters before Vitus.
On the street of angels
lives a grandma. Maybe Esther...
September has gone crazy—
it smells of fires and...flowers.
Too late, Esther, too late to intercede for the people!
... The frightened beehive of a street
    fell apart in an instant.
Liuteranska Street was and remains
    a ribbon on the body of the city,
a seam in the background of inevitability.
Slowly, I discernthe shadow of a German colonist.
German?! I feel numb from this scary coincidence.
And again the street runs down
    into the embraces of Khreshchatyk,
clearing the way to Calvary.
On this shortest longest road
nothing can be distinguished today,
except for a bakery on the corner.
And I still don't know what I should do with my eyes—
I'm hiding in a shell of nonparticipation.
Grandma, Grandma, step in!
Everyone here is your child...
You can't fly, street, you can't fly,
you need to stop that rockfall, timefall, painfall.
Crawl, Liuteranska Street, crawl!
You're a street of rage, you're a deadly wound.

Ім'я твоє розривається навпіл,
    в бабусиних гасне очах.
Це навіть не сепія, навіть не чорне та біле.
    Це вже поза снами вогких кольорів,
поза всесвітом барв.

2016

Your name is being torn in half,
it fades out in the grandma's eyes.
It's not even sepia, it's not even black and white.
It's already beyond the dreams of damp colors,
beyond the universe of colors.

2016

Oleksa Iushchenko (1917–2008) was a poet, children's writer, and journalist. In the course of his lifetime, over thirty volumes of his writings appeared. During World War II, he worked at a radio station that broadcast throughout the occupied zones of Soviet Ukraine. After the Red Army recaptured Kyiv, he returned to the city with the apparatus of the radio station and took up residence there.

Бабин Яр

На безлистих, дрібних кущах
Вранці хустка тріпоче, біліє,
Жмут волосся, коса чорніє...
А чиї ж то кості в ровах?
По смутних, по осінніх ночах
То ж по кому все тужить птах?
Бабин яр, чорний яр, смерті яр,
Пропливають тіні примар...
Виглядає з піску черевик —
От розсиплеться, як пісок.
Тут останній дитини крок,
Материний невтішний крик.
Ой околиця, де недоля ця...
З жаху серце чиє не розколеться?
Хто, побачивши, не здригнеться?
В серці бурею відгукнеться:
На безлистих дрібних кущах
Там он хустка тріпоче, біліє,
Жмут волосся — коса чорніє...
А чиї ж то кості в ровах?
Бабин яр, чорний яр, смерті яр,
Над ним стеляться тіні примар.
Душогуби, заброди розлючені,
Скільки, скільки вони замучили...
Дні захмарені, дні затучені
Як ридали сльозами кипучими,
...Мордували, стріляли тут, мучили...
Цвинтар мучеників. Тишина.
Та прислухайсь —
рида хтось, кона?

Babyn Yar

In the morning, on the leafless shrubs
A kerchief flutters, turns white,
A clump of hair, a braid turns black...
But whose bones are in the ravines?
During the sad, autumnal night
For whom does a bird yearn?
Babyn Yar, a black ravine, a death ravine,
The shadows of specters sail by...
A shoe pokes out from the sand—
It will dissolve like sand.
Here is the last step of a child,
A mother's grieving scream.
The outskirts where this misfortune...
Whose heart will not break from terror?
Who, upon seeing, will not shudder?
It will resonate in the heart like a storm:
In the morning, on the leafless shrubs
A kerchief flutters, turns white,
A clump of hair, a braid turns black...
But whose bones are in the ravines?
Babyn Yar, a black ravine, a death ravine,
Above them spread the shadows of specters.
Murderers, savage foreigners,
How many, how many did they torture...
There were clouds, the days were overcast
As they wept profusely,
... They murdered here, shot, tortured...
The cemetery of martyrs. Silence.
But listen—
                Is someone weeping, dying?

І здригнеться Лук'янівка наче —
Цвинтар кров'ю невинною плаче...
Чуєш, яр, закривавлений яр, —
Не втекли душогуби від згуби,
Не втекли від покар!

1944

And Luk'ianivka is shaking as though—
The cemetery weeps innocent blood...
You hear, ravine, bloody ravine—
The murderers did not escape death,
They did not escape punishment!

1944

Igor Kaczurowskyj (1918–2013) was a poet, translator, fiction writer, literary scholar and journalist. In 1943 he left Ukraine and settled in Austria in 1945. In 1948, he immigrated to Argentina and settled down in Buenos Aires. In 1969, he moved to Munich and worked as a literary observer for Radio Liberty/Radio Free Europe in the 1970s and 1980s. In 1973, he began teaching at the Ukrainian Free University in Munich. His debut poetry collection appeared in 1948; his last collection, *Liryka* (Lyrics), was published in 2013. In addition to poetry, he published many books of prose, translations, and scholarly works.

Марті Тарнавській

(Відгук на поезію «В житті моєму...»)

Ще багрянів, як рана, Бабин Яр,
А вже пішли прочісувати Київ.
І містом плив яріючий кошмар
У випарах кривавих чорториїв.

Замало жертв — не всі тоді зійшлись:
Хто сам утік, кого сховали люди.
...Випитували хижо: «Юде? Юде?»
І переможно нишпорили скрізь.

У шафи і під ліжка зазирали...
Ніхто з них Ґете, певно, не читав,
Про Ваґнера ніхто не пам'ятав,
Обходячи горища і підвали.

Ввалились і в квартиру-ательє,
Де віяв дух Шпіцвеґа й Фраґонара,
І Франца Гальса, й Ґойї, й Ренуара,
Що в кожнім з них містична сила є.

І втупились в картини і мольберти —
І стихли зачудовано нараз,
Немов перед закляттям проти смерті:
— Пробачте! Ми не потурбуєм вас...

З катівськими ознаками на шапці
Так несполучні ввічливі слова...
...А в шафі в них тремтіла, ледь жива,
Стара еврейка, приятелька бабці.

1982

To Marta Tarnawsky

(A response to her poem "In my life too...")

Babyn Yar was still bleeding, a wound,
Though they'd already set out to search Kyiv.
And terror flowed through the city
In the vapors above the blood-soaked ravines.

Not enough victims—not everyone had arrived:
Some escaped; others, people hid.
...They were asking viciously: "Jude? Jude?"
And triumphantly searching everywhere.

They looked in closets and under beds...
Most likely none of them had read Goethe,
And nobody remembered any Wagner
While raiding attics and basements.

They also burst into an atelier where
The spirit of Spitzweg and Fragonard hovered,
And of Frans Hals, and Goya, and Renoir,
Each of whom possessed a mystical power.

And they stopped at once, suddenly,
And stared at the paintings and easels
As if enchanted by the spell of death:
"Forgive us! We won't bother you again..."

The symbols of torture on their caps
Were so incompatible with those polite words...
...And in the closet trembled, barely alive,
An old Jewish woman, my grandmother's friend.

1982

Abram Katsnel′son (1914–2003) was a poet, translator, and literary critic. His first collection of poetry was published in 1935. He authored many poetry collections and collections of essays during the Soviet era. In August 1994 Katsnel′son moved to the United States and lived the rest of his life in Los Angeles. After moving to the United States, he published several collections of poetry. His essays range thematically from poetry studies to the analysis of poetic language.

У Бабинім Яру

Спинились біля яру,
що здавна звався
«Бабин».
Був першим у колоні старий
колишній рабин.
З манатками дрібними в незвідану дорогу
узяв ярмулку, та́лес,
щоб десь молитись
Богу.
Коли ж відчув загибель,
за п'ять хвилин до згуби
молитву шепотіли його поблідлі губи.
А смерть йому у вічі як глянула зловіщо,
до неба скинув руки:
«Ой готеню, за віщо?..»
Та сухо тріснув постріл —
і в глинищі зостались
і рабин, і ярмулка, і в плямах крові талес…

1990

In Babyn Yar

They arrived at the ravine
that had been called Babyn Yar
for a long time.
The first in the column
was an old rabbi.
Along with his meager possessions,
on this unknown journey he took
a yarmulke and tallis to pray to God
somewhere on the way.
When he had a premonition of death
five minutes before the end
his pale lips whispered a prayer.
And death peered into his eyes ominously,
he threw his hands to the sky:
"Oh gotenyu, what did I do?..."
And a shot dryly cracked—
and in the clay remained
a rabbi, yarmulke, and tallis covered in blood...

1990

Монолог онука

В Яр піду і поклонюся.
Він — здалося так мені —
зветься «Бабин», що бабуся,
наша бабця Рейзл-Буся,
мертва там лежить на дні.

Ми її любили, внуки,
найпочеснішу в сім'ї,
вузлуваті її руки,
мудру посмішку її.
Завжди лагідна і тиха,
ні краплини в неї зла.

Прожила й нікому лиха
і образ не завдала.
Прикриваючи обличчя
крильцями тонких долонь,
як обожнювала свічі,
їхній трепетний вогонь!
То вона нечутно з Богом
розмовляла в сяйві свіч,
щастя бідним і убогим
в ту вимолювала ніч.

...В Яр піду і поклонюся.
Він — здалося так мені —
зветься «Бабин», що бабуся,
наша бабця Рейзл-Буся,
мертва там лежить на дні.

1990

Grandson's Monologue

I'll go to the ravine and bow down.
It's called—it seems to me—
Babyn Yar, "grandma's ravine,"
and our grandma Reizl-Busia
lies there dead down below.

We, her grandsons, love her,
the most honorable in our family,
her knotty hands,
her knowing smile.
Always gentle and quiet,
not a drop of evil in her.

She lived and didn't cause anyone
trouble, didn't offend anyone.
Covering her face
with the wings of her thin palms,
how she adored candles,
their quivering fire!
She talked silently with God
in the candlelight,
that night she prayed for joy
for the poor and crippled.

... I'll go to the ravine and bow down.
It's called—it seems to me—
Babyn Yar, "grandma's ravine,"
and our grandma Reizl-Busia
lies there dead down below.

1990

Київ. 29 вересня. Бабин Яр

Осіння, пам'ятна,
в жалобі чорна ніч.
У Бабинім Яру
палають сотні свіч.
Сльозами сліпить зір
незримий дим гіркий.
Поблідли в небесах
від жаху всі зірки.

1990

Kyiv. September 29. Babyn Yar

A black fall night,
memorable, full of mourning.
In Babyn Yar
hundreds of candles burn.
Bitter invisible smoke
blinds vision with tears.
All the stars in the sky
have gone pale from terror.

1990

Marianna Kiyanovska (b. 1973) is a poet, writer, translator, and literary scholar. She is the author of many collections of poetry and one collection of short stories. She has translated poems from Polish, Lithuanian and Belarussian into Ukrainian. Kiyanovska is the recipient of prestigious awards including the Kyiv Laurels Literary Festival Prize (2011) and the Taras Shevchenko Prize for poetry (2020). In 2014, Forbes Ukraine named her one of the top ten most influential writers working in Ukraine. A collection of her poems in English translation, *The Voices of Babyn Yar*, was published by the Harvard Ukrainian Research Institute in 2022. She lives and works in Lviv.

[я би вмерла на вулиці цій або тій що за рогом]

я би вмерла на вулиці цій або тій що за рогом
та конвой не дозволить здається проси не проси
у валізі не те щоби речі збиралась в дорогу
як збираються люди в дорогу в останні часи
тільки ключ і листи фотографії брошка і гроші
ну не те щоби гроші всього лише кілька банкнот
ми бредемо по куряві літній немов по пороші
оминаючи вирви тіла і сліди нечистот
увірвалися в дім наказали все цінне узяти
я взяла теплий плед трохи хліба і трохи води
а есесівець крививсь віспаво на вбогість кімнати
що запалася раптом в ніщо як і я назавжди
а тепер я іду назавжди розумію і бачу
всю приреченість нашу крізь світла щільного ясу
я би вмерла на вулиці цій і тому я не плачу
а валізу на брук опускаю ім’я лиш несу
я рахиля

2017

[i would die on this street or on the one around the corner]

i would die on this street or
    on the one around the corner
but the convoy won't let me it seems
    whether you beg or not
unusual things in my suitcase i've packed
the way people pack for the road these days
only the key letters photographs a brooch and money
all right not exactly money just a few bills
we wander through the summer dust
    as through first snow
bypassing the craters bodies and the traces of sewage
they burst into the house and ordered us
    to take all valuables
i took a warm blanket some bread and some water
and an ss soldier grimaced at the poverty of our room
which suddenly fell into nothing like me into forever
and now i'm leaving for good i understand and see
all our doom through the glitter of intense lights
i would die on this street and so i don't cry
but i settle my suitcase on cobblestones i carry
    only my name
i'm rakhel

2017

[за цю війну я навіть аж підріс]

за цю війну я навіть аж підріс
ходив у другий клас тепер я був би
у третьому болить розбитий ніс
ударив срулік я про це й забув би
якби не те що ми із ним удвох
вціліли чудом із цілого класу
я заховався за чортополох
він ніч сидів на дереві щоразу
зригався і боявся що впаде
від страху весь спітнів казав до нитки
він думав хтось лишився та ніде
нікого але в їхньої сусідки
знайшовся кусник хліба на столі
він дав його мені казав не хоче
бо всіх убили всі лежать в землі
у бабинім яру земля хлюпоче
казав від крові там живих катма
вбивати німців в нього є граната
вже третій день його ніде нема
дивлюсь на жовті стрілки циферблата
годинник дідів і давно не йде
я скоро вмру як він бо час не жде
бо як була облава всіх взяли
й мене візьмуть не знаю ще коли

2017

[i even managed to grow during the war]

i even managed to grow during the war
i went to second grade now i would have been
in the third my broken nose hurts
srulik punched me i would have even forgotten about it
if not for the fact that he and i
miraculously survived out of the whole class
i hid among thistle
he sat the whole night in a tree every time
he shivered i was afraid he would fall down
out of fear he was all sweaty he said soaked to the skin
he thought others survived but no one
nowhere but at his neighbor's
he found a piece of bread on the table
he gave it to me saying he didn't want it
because all were killed all lying in the ground
in babyn yar the earth soaked
he said with blood there are few survivors
to kill germans he has a grenade
he's nowhere to be found for the third day
i look at the yellow arrow on the face
of my grandpa's watch and it hasn't worked for a while
i will die soon like him because time doesn't wait
because during the raid everyone was taken
and i will be taken i don't know when

2017

[я все ж таки це промовлю я все ж таки це прийму]

я все ж таки це промовлю я все ж таки це прийму
сказавши і не сказавши неначе ввійду у море
війна означає безвість і болю страшну пітьму
і ще означає відчай і голе коротке горе
я був на дніпрі учора насправді не на дніпрі
а просто здаля дивився на води його і хвилі
горіло рудаве листя дерев і човни старі
ховалися під водою і гнили і чайки білі
даремно шукали свідка на свій непташиний крик
оплакуючи рибалок і просто загибель міста
і я заридав нелюдськи та був прикусив язик
а зараз я це промовлю: присутність завжди двоїста
просвердлені намистини ми:
        хтось кулею наскрізь хтось
нанизані намистини ми і жодна не є окремо
і сонце стоїть так високо немов воно піднялось
щоб місто згори побачити і як ми у ньому мремо
і як ми у ньому ходимо дивитися на ріку
тому що нас убивають аделька мір'ям дебора
лежать у яру розстріляні я маю печаль таку
що серце зробилось каменем і стала душа прозора
і тоншає все і тоншає а це означає смерть
і сутність її двоїста бо смерть це насправді разом
з аделькою і деборою з мір'ям доки неба твердь
і доки дніпро і кручі у досвідах поза часом

2017

[i will say it anyway
i will accept it anyway]

i will say it anyway i will accept it anyway
by articulating it or not as if i walked into the sea
war means not knowing
        and the terrible darkness of pain
and it also means despair and naked bursts of grief
i was on the dnipro yesterday actually not on the dnipro
just looking from afar at its water and waves
red leaves of trees burning and old boats
sunk beneath the water and decomposing
        and white seagulls
seeking a witness in vain for the first non-bird's scream
mourning fishermen and the destruction of the city
and i wept inhumanly and bit my tongue
but now i will say it: presence is always twofold
we're drilled beads: one with a bullet one clean through
we're stringed beads and none is separate
and the sun stands high as if it had climbed up
to see the city from above and how we're dying in it
and how we walk in it to look at the river
because we are being killed adele miriam deborah
lie in the ravine shot i have such grief
that my heart has become stone
        and my soul transparent
and it gets thinner and thinner and this means death
and its essence is twofold because death means
        being together
with adel and deborah and miriam until the sky is solid
and until the dnipro and its cliffs are experienced
        beyond time

2017

[ці вулиці вже руїни
ще може не всі та вже]

ці вулиці вже руїни ще може не всі та вже
я це кістьми відчуваю мені це болить у жилах
і небо таке глибоке і сонце таке чуже
і тяжко іти під гору...
казали...
в ровах-могилах...
казали... в ровах-могилах... між вбитих... напівживі...
і стогнуть рови ночами... цей стогін у тиші чути
на кілька сусідніх вулиць як шелести у траві
як гухання і як регіт який розриває груди
казали що у будинках жидівських всуціль скарби
тепер їх всуціль простукують і часто сусіди всякі
і стукіт цей також чути на вулицях і якби
каміння могло кричати воно би кричало яків
упав і його пристрелили в колоні не всі за всіх
не кожен тебе підтримає не кожен візьме за руку
та може воно і добре із яру безтямний сміх
а потім коротка черга здіймає з землі пилюку
не знає скорбот людина не знає скорботи місць
не знає дороги серця аж доки не вийде з часу
а я... помежи ровами... лежатиму... добрий гість...
і з мене ростиме дерево безмежно живе щоразу

2017

[these streets are already ruins maybe not all but already]

these streets are already ruins maybe not all but already
i feel it with my bones it hurts me in my veins
and the sky is so deep and the sun is so alien
and it's so hard to get uphill...
they said...
in ravine-graves...
they said... in ravine-graves... among the murdered...
some are half-dead...
and the ravines moan at night... in the quiet you hear
the moaning
on several neighborhood streets like the rustling in the grass
like a sudden sound and like laughter that splits
the chest open
they said that the jewish houses were full of treasures
now they're sounding the walls and floors
and often various neighbors
and this knocking is also heard on the streets and if
the stones could scream they would scream yakiv
fell down and was shot there in a column it's not one for all
not everyone will hold you up not everyone
will take your hand
but maybe it's for the better from the ravine
delirious laughter
and then a short round of gunfire raises dust
from the ground
humans don't know sorrow don't know the sorrow
of these places
don't know the heart's road until they walk out of time
and i... among the ravines... will lie... a good guest...
and out of me will grow a tree enormously alive always

2017

[збираю колекцію три найостанніші тижні]

збираю колекцію три найостанніші тижні
описую всі фотознімки братів зокрема
щоденники свій і аркашин нотатник колишні
розхристані спогади нинішніх в мене нема
складаю в коробку листи і сестри рукоділля
засушені квіти марія сказала б траву
сьогодні ще трохи посплю завтра буде неділя
а потім вівторок звичайно якщо доживу
усе що я можу занести це все на горище
і хай би цей мотлох знайшли може дім як знесуть
хотів би лишити в кімнаті та думаю вище
її не пожбурять в сміття адже в тому вся суть
загибель помпеї спочатку лиш лава і м'ясо
гаряче людське а тепер це музей і скарби
у києві сталося щось не з жидами а з часом
у часі не стало майбутнього в часі доби
не стало години на спокій війна і облави
тіла на дорозі на тиньку подекуди кров
ходжу тепер тільки до наді питаю як справи
кажу їй дивися я тут бути поруч любов
я йду ризикуючи тілом якого не стане
до тебе щоб просто посидіти мовчки удвох
спаси і помилуй молюся та слово осанни
стає тільки словом врятуй я не знаю чи бог
врятує мене і надію та знаю достоту

[i've been getting together a collection for the last three weeks]

i've been getting together a collection the last three weeks
i'm labeling all the photographs
    of the brothers in particular
the diaries mine and arkasha's notebook old
scattered memories i don't have any recent ones
i put letters in the box and my sister's handmade things
dried flowers maria would have called grass
today i will get some more sleep tomorrow is sunday
and then tuesday of course if i live till then
all i can do is put everything in the attic
and let them find this junk maybe when
    the house is demolished
i would like to leave it in my room but i think it won't be
dumped in the trash if it's up there
    because that's the point
the death of pompeii at first lava and hot
human flesh and now they're museum pieces
    and treasures
in kyiv something happened with time not with the jews
time has no future anymore and there is no time
today for rest war and raids
bodies along the road sometimes blood on the fence
now i only go to see nadia i ask how she's doing
i tell her look i'm here to be near means love
i walk to you risking my body which won't exist
just so the two of us can sit silently
save us and have mercy i'm praying but the prayer
becomes only save us i don't know if god
will save me and nadia but I know for sure

що скарб на горищі це наші в майбутнє сліди
роблю непомітну дрібну і невдячну роботу
простого втривалення пам'ять про нас назавжди
не знаю чи житиму потім бо зле воно всюди
облави щокожного дня і жахіття як сни
я був у помпеях дитиною пам'ять це люди
а іноді речі а іноді рештки стіни
якби я умів умирати я вмер би можливо
я знаю напевно що вже незабаром умру
збираю колекцію боже мій пам'ять це диво
усе що я маю сім'я всіх убили в яру

2017

that treasures in the attic are our footprints into the future
i do inconspicuous small and unappreciated work
simply inscribing memory of us into forever
i don't know if i will survive because it's so bad everywhere
raids every day and horrors like dreams
i was in pompeii as a child memory is people
and sometimes things and sometimes parts of a wall
if i only knew how to die I would probably die
i know for sure that I will die soon
i work on the collection my god memory is a miracle
all i have is a family all were killed in the ravine

2017

[ось яр у якому розстрілює ганс]

ось яр у якому розстрілює ганс
ось гільзи від куль що влучають у нас
ось сліди і відбитки кулемета і ніг
ганс замучився стих
неможливо щоб всіх
хтось би може піднявсь хтось би може побіг
але куно вихаркує чергу і сміх
ось фріц коло ривки зо три рани але
ось обручка сережки все занадто мале
ось обличчя її золоте все життя
ось великий живіт і в утробі дитя
ривка чує усе навіть серцебиття
фріц стріляє в живіт і говорить: сміття
ось альберт брат убитого йони єврей
ось під нігтями в нього дві скалки з дверей
ось червоний рубець на обличчі блідім
сара квилила йдемо ходімо ходім
він чіплявсь за одвірок хапався за дім
він хотів би і жити і вмерти у нім
але ось він у ямі і рідні із ним
ось роздертий рукав тобто слід рукава
ось брунатна від крові земля і трава
ось тіла і тіла і тіла і тіла
ось мір’ям молода що щаслива була
ось її обіймає вже мертва мала
бідна циля і гріє теплом без тепла
ось над яром густа і рожева імла

2017

[here is the ravine where hans does his shooting]

here is the ravine where hans does his shooting
here are the shells of bullets that are hitting us
here are traces of a machine gun and footprints
hans got tired and went silent
it's impossible that everyone
someone might have gotten up someone might have run
but kuno is spitting out another round and laughter
here is fritz near rivka some three wounds but
here is an engagement ring earrings everything is too small
here is her golden face all her life
here is her big belly and a baby in her womb
rivka hears everything even the heartbeat
fritz shoots her in the belly and says: garbage
here is albert brother of the murdered yona a jew
here are two splinters from the door under his fingernails
here is a red scar on his pale face
sara wails let's go let's go let's go
he clung to the doorpost grabbed onto the house
he wanted to live and die there
but here he is in the ravine and his relatives are with him
here is a torn sleeve actually a bit of the sleeve
here is blood-stained soil and grass
here are bodies and bodies and bodies and bodies
here is young miriam who was happy
here she is being embraced by poor small
dead tsylia who warms her up with warmth without warmth
here is a thick and pink mist above the ravine

2017

Dmytro Pavlychko (b. 1929) is a poet, translator, and political activist. In the Soviet and post-Soviet eras, Pavlychko has been one of Ukraine's most widely recognized poets and received the most prestigious literary awards. From 1971 to 1978 he was editor-in-chief of the influential literary journal *Vsesvit*. More than twenty volumes of his works have been published in the period between the 1950s and the 2020s. His collection of selected poetry in English translation, *Two Colors of Love*, was published in 2013. Pavlychko presently lives in Kyiv.

[Ходивши біля Бабиного Яру]

Ходивши біля Бабиного Яру,
Де плаче вітер сивий, як пророк,
Я на червоний наступив листок,
Що з клена впав на плити тротуару.

І бризнула, як полум'я пожару,
Із нього кров, і послизнувся крок.
Озвався кулемет, і в темний зморок.
Неначе в яму, впав я від удару.

Там я помер від кулі і воскрес,
Але навік, як блискавка шалена,
В душі моїй зостався крик небес.

Вступила в мене сила незнищенна,
А наді мною листя, як знамена,
Палало в глибині небесних плес.

1976

[Walking near Babyn Yar]

Walking near Babyn Yar
Where the grey wind cries like a prophet,
I stepped on a red leaf
That fell on the sidewalk from a maple tree.

And blood burst out of it like
A fire's flame, and my foot slipped.
A machine gun rattled, and into pitch dark
As if into a pit I fell, hammered from a blow.

There I died from a bullet and was resurrected,
But the roar of heaven remained in my soul
For good, like a mad lightning bolt.

An indestructible force entered my body,
And above me the leaves, like banners,
Burned in the depths of vast stretches of sky.

1976

[Край Бабиного Яру в небеса]

Край Бабиного Яру в небеса
Звелася телевежа. А під нею
Сіяння дивне стелеться землею,
Немов осінніх яворів яса...

Та ні! Там сяє мамина сльоза
Крізь товщу закривавленого глею,
Там біле світло, схоже на лілею,
Запалює блакить, як та гроза.

А там димують гори, наче рани,
Вкриваються вогнем материки,
Болінням людства світять океани.

Куди ж те сяйво лине? Де зірки,
Що повертають на свої екрани
Забитих душ невигаслі думки?!

1977

[On the edge of Babyn Yar they raised]

On the edge of Babyn Yar they raised
A TV tower to the heavens. Beyond it
A strange radiance extends across the ground,
Like the flame of ash trees in the fall.

But wait! There a mother's tears shine
Through layers of bloodsoaked clay,
And there, light as white as a lily
Brightens the blue sky like a thunderstorm.

And there, mountains covered in smoke, like wounds,
The continents are consumed by fire,
And oceans gleam with human pain.

Where does this shining lead? Where are
The stars that return to their screens
The imperishable thoughts of murdered souls?

1977

Реквієм. Бабин Яр

1

Владико світла, доброти і правди,
Зійди з небес, на землю нашу стань.
Тут людська кров пролита без пощади,
Горить в могилі як незгасна грань.

Втиши плачі і зойки в тьмі глибокій,
Серця розбиті ласкою вгорни;
Даруй святому праху вічний спокій.
Благословенні, непробудні сни.

2

Ми тут лежимо в піску на глеї,
На всі сторони світу простерті —
Євреї, євреї, євреї —
Діди, матері, немовлята.
Господи, дай нам відпочити від смерті,
Від погляду ката!

3

Буде суд і буде кара,
Отверзеться Бабин Яр,
Хлине кров як повінь яра,
Вдарить хвиля аж до хмар.

На узвишшя піднебесне
Вийде світлий судія.

Requiem for Babyn Yar

1

Lord of light, kindness, and truth,
Come down from heaven, walk our earth.
Human blood is spilled here without mercy,
Sears the grave, inextinguishable margin.

Calm the crying and howling in darkness,
Heal broken hearts with grace;
Give eternal peace to the holy ashes,
Blessed, uninterrupted dreams.

2

We lie here in the sand and clay,
Aimed at all parts of the world,
Jews, Jews, Jews.
Grandfathers, mothers, infants.
Lord, let us rest from death,
From the glance of the executioner!

3

There will be judgment and punishment,
Babyn Yar will open up,
Blood will flood the ravine,
A wave will rise to the clouds.

A luminous judge will step down
Atop a celestial hill.

Крикнуть сурми і воскресне
Вся Давидова сім'я.

Не сховається почвара,
Ані вбивця, ні грабар.
Буде суд і буде кара,
Отверзеться Бабин Яр.

Розпадуться небосхили,
Божа явиться могуть.
Вийдуть праведні з могили,
Злих в могилу поведуть.

4

Боже, ти створив людину,
Дух вселив у темну глину—
Для добра й святого чину.
Людству дав ти в нагороду
Власну мудрість, власну вроду,
Заповів братерство й згоду.
Чом же ми, твої творіння,
Повні смертного терпіння,
В землю вбиті, мов каміння?

Та невже твою подобу
Мали й ті, що нас до гробу
Поскидали, мов худобу?
Не над нашою судьбою,
Не над людською ганьбою—
Зглянься, Боже, над собою!
Зглянься над самим собою!

The trumpets will sound
And David's whole family resurrect.

The monster won't be able to hide,
Nor the killer, nor the gravedigger.
There will be judgment and punishment,
Babyn Yar will open up.

The skies will break apart,
God's power will be revealed.
The righteous dead will be raised
And lead the wicked to the grave.

4

Lord, you created man,
You imbued dark clay with spirit
For holy and righteous deeds.
You rewarded humanity with
Your wisdom and your beauty,
Commanded brotherhood and peace.
Why are we, your creatures,
Full of mortal patience,
Ground into the earth like stones?

Did those who threw us
Into the grave like cattle
Bear your resemblance?
Forget our fate,
Our human disgrace—
Show yourself kindness, God,
Show yourself mercy!

5

Похилений вітром осіннім,
Над Бабиним Яром стою.
Отця сивобрового бачу,
І брата, і матір свою.

Не тут вони тяжко вмирали,
Не тут вони зморені сплять.
Та їхні молитви й благання
В деревах десь тут шелестять.

Тут Київ та рід мій козацький,
Тут наша свобода в крові.
Над братнім усопшим народом
Ми молимось, мертві й живі.

Я бачу — то мамині сльози
Блискочуть на хвилях Дніпра.
Я знаю — моя Україна
Воскресне на поклик добра!

6

Господи, за що нам ця спокута —
Куля гітлерівська гостра й люта!

А за що загнали разом з нами
Непорочних діточок до ями?
Згасла в небі наша мить остання,
Та не згасли стогони й волання.
Наші скарги, голоси засмути —
Доки світу й сонця — буде чути!

5

Bent by the autumn wind,
I'm standing above Babyn Yar.
I see my gray-haired father,
My mother, and my brother.

They didn't die in pain here,
They don't sleep here tortured.
But their prayers and supplications
Rustle somewhere here in the trees.

Here's Kyiv and my Cossack kin.
Here's our freedom covered in blood.
We pray, the lost and the living,
For our fraternal dead.

I see my mother's tears
Reflected on the waves of the Dnipro.
I know my Ukraine will be
Resurrected by the call to goodness!

6

Lord, this redemption, Hitler's bullet,
Sharp and fierce—what's it for?
And why do they shove innocent
Children into the ravine with us?
Our final moment faded in the sky,
But the groaning and crying continued.
Our complaints, the voices of sorrow—
As long as there's world and sun—will be heard!

7

Мойсею сивий, гнаний до рова,
Пекла вогнем душа твоя жива,
Твоя печаль крушила серце звіра.
Ти гордо над безоднею стояв,
Руками дітям очі затуляв,
Йдучи на смерть як Господу офіра.

Здирали одяг з тебе, як з Христа,
Та в погляді твоїм була не мста,
А лиш розпука та сумна докора.
Так, наче бачив ти нову скрижаль
Де людству накарбована печаль —
Будущина несправедлива й хвора.

Невже лилась невинна кров задарма,
Невже будяччя вкриє Бабин Яр,
І новий цар заб'є народи в ярма?
Ні, відсахнеться смерті хижий сон,
Розвалиться новітній Вавилон! —
Возрадуйся! — Ти не помер задарма!

8

Возрадуйтеся з нами,
Невинно вбиті,
Прилучені смертю своєю
До творителя доброти.
В совісті людства сяючі
Наче сонце в блакиті,
В праведних душах сущі,
Невмирущі мої брати!

7

Grey Moses, you were rushed to the ravine,
Your living soul burnt with fire,
Your sorrow broke the heart of a beast.
You stood proudly over the abyss,
Covering the children's eyes with your hands,
Going to death like God's sacrifice.

They stripped you of your clothes, like Christ,
But there was no vengeance in your glance,
Only calamity and a sad reproach.
It's as if you saw a new stone tablet,
Humanity engraved with sorrow—
The future is unfair and vile.

Was innocent blood spilled for nothing,
Will thistles cover Babyn Yar
And a new tsar yoke the people to their burden?
No, the dreadful dream of death will wither,
This new Babylon will fall apart!—
—Rejoice! You didn't die for nothing!

8

Rejoice with us,
You, killed for no crime,
You're attached through death
To the creator of kindness.
My immortal brothers,
You exist in righteous souls!
You shine like the sun in azure
In the consciousness of humanity.

9

Великий Боже, ми з твоєї згоди
Проходимо дорогу в Бабин Яр,
Де смертю ти поєднуєш народи,
Щоб зберегти життя й свободи дар.

Втиши плачі і зойки в тьмі глибокій,
Серця розбиті ласкою вгорни.
Даруй святому праху вічний спокій,
Благословенні, непробудні сни!

1991

9

Great God, with your permission we
Take the road to Babyn Yar,
Where you unite people through death
To save lives and preserve the gift of freedom.

Calm the crying and howling in darkness,
Heal broken hearts with grace,
Give eternal peace to the holy ashes,
Blessed, uninterrupted dreams.

1991

Leonid Pervomais′kyi (1908–73) was a poet, writer, and translator. He moved to Kharkiv in 1926 and worked there as an editor for newspapers, journals, and various publishing houses. From 1934 to 1941 he lived in Kyiv. The most complete edition of Pervomais′kyi's works is *Tvory. U semy tomakh* (Works in seven volumes, 1985–86). Pervomais′kyi translated the works of S. Petőfi, Heinrich Heine, François Villon, Federico Garcia Lorca, and other writers.

[Воскреси мене, майбутнє, для нового]

Воскреси мене, майбутнє, для нового
Існування на новім віку.
Пильно глянь на мене, на живого,
В темному іржавому вінку—

Не в терновому, а з того дроту,
Що перетинає білий світ,
На терпіння ділячи й підлоту
На убивць і жертви людський рід.

Я в житті пройшов таку Голгофу
Через яр до ближньої соші,
Що мої хлюпочуть кров'ю строфи
Й стигми не зростаються в душі.

Я в юрбі стояв на кладовищі
Голий поміж нагробків і між плит,
Згадуючи пориви найвищі,
Світ без болю і без крові світ.

І коли я падав мертвий з кручі
В глинище кривавих тіл страшне,
Вперто вірив я, що неминуче
Прийдеш ти, щоб воскресить мене.

Воскреси ж мене, коли ти в вічі
Чесно можеш глянути мені,—
Я для тебе жив в такім сторіччі,
Що таких уже не буде, ні...

[Resurrect me, future, for a new]

Resurrect me, future, for a new
Existence in a new time.
Look at me attentively, alive,
In my dark, rusty crown—

Not of thorns but made from that wire
That bisects the immaculate world,
Dividing it into patience and villainy,
Human beings, into killers and victims.

In my life, I passed such a Golgotha
Through a ravine to a nearby road
So my stanzas are wet with blood
And the wounds in my soul won't heal.

I stood in a crowd at the cemetery,
Naked, among tombstones and markers,
Remembering the wonderful times,
The world without pain and blood.

And when I was falling down, dead, from a cliff
Into the terrifying rot of bloody bodies,
I believed tenaciously that you'd inevitably
Come to resurrect me.

Resurrect me, if you can
Honestly look me in the eye—
I've lived for you through a century
That will not happen again, ever.

Воскреси ж мене в житті, де чорних
Струм не перепалює на прах,
Де не перемелюють на жорнах
Людський попіл по міських ярах.

Воскреси хоча б на мить єдину,
Щоб в'яву побачити я міг
Чесний хліб, який живить людину
На столі голодних і німих.

Воскреси мене в лугах зелених
Серед квітів і похилих трав,
Щоб могли живі сказать про мене,
Що я також смертю смерть поправ.

Воскреси рядком, єдиним словом,
Хай воно прошелестить в траві
І далеким ранком малиновим
Вріжеться в нові серця живі.

А коли й в тобі нема надії,
Як в минулих не було віках,
Хай зо мною цей рядок зотліє
І у мертвих згубиться пісках.

1964

Resurrect me into a life where bodies
Are not transfigured into ash,
Where millstones don't grind
Human ashes in the city's ravines.

Resurrect me at least for a second,
So I can see the real world,
Honest bread, which feeds a human,
On the table of the hungry and deaf.

Resurrect me on green meadows
Among flowers and wilted grass
So that the living can say
That I trampled death with death, too.

Resurrect me as a line, a sole word,
Let it rustle in the grass
And crash into living hearts
Some remote raspberry dawn.

And when even you have no hope,
Just as there was no hope in the past,
Let this line rot with me
And vanish in the sand.

1964

В Бабинім Яру

Стань біля мене, стань, мій сину,
Я прикрию долонею твої очі,
Щоб ти не побачив своєї смерті,
А тільки кров мою в пальцях на сонці,
Ту кров, що й твоєю стала кров'ю
І зараз вилитись має на землю...

1968

At Babyn Yar

Stand near me, stand close, my son,
I will cover your eyes with my hand
So you don't see your death,
But only the blood on my fingers in the sun,
That blood that became yours too
And is about to spill on the ground...

1968

Volodymyr Pidpalyi (1936–72) was a poet, editor, and translator. He studied at the Kyiv University and later worked as an editor at the publishing house Radians´kyi pys´mennyk (Soviet writer). Pidpalyi authored the following collections: *Zelena hilka* (Green bunch, 1963), *Trydtsiate lito* (The thirtieth summer, 1967), *V dorohu—za lastivkamy* (Hit the road, follow the swallows; 1968), *Vyshnevyi svit* (Cherry world, 1970). Several more collections were published posthumously: *Syni troiandy* (Blue roses, 1979), *Poezii̇̈* (Poems, 1982), *Zoloti dzhmeli* (Golden bumblebees, 2011).

Бабин Яр

У Бабин яр!.. А там джерела
водою крижаною б'ють,
у синім небі каравели
бездомних хмар пливуть
і пропливають без печалі
за сум, за суть, за сміх...
На тихі вечорів скрижалі
слів не стає моїх.
Отут заснути без печалі,
сказавши все, що міг...

1972

Babyn Yar

To Babyn Yar!... There springs
erupt with ice-cold water.
In the blue sky the caravels
of homeless clouds steer by,
and they sail without grief
beyond sorrow, meaning, laughter...
I don't have the words
for the quiet scrolls of evening.
If only I could fall asleep here without grief
after having told you everything...

1972

Maksym Ryl's'kyi (1895–1964) was one of the most important poets of the twentieth century in Ukrainian literature. He was closely associated with the Neoclassicist group. Ryl's'kyi was a prolific translator from English, French, German, and Polish, as well as a folklore and literary scholar. Twenty volumes of his works appeared posthumously in the 1980s. An English translation of his work appeared as *The Selected Lyric Poetry of Maksym Rylsky* in 2017.

Єврейському народові

Народе, що землі дав геніїв великих,
Народе, що несеш із вікових глибин,
Високий, чесний дух серед обмовин диких,—
Низький тобі уклін!

Нас хліб живив один, одні поїли води.
Ділили, як брати, ми радість і печаль,
І нам за землю цю, за цвіт її свободи
Життя віддать не жаль.

Знов щастя навкруги простелеться безкрайнє,
В кривавій боротьбі йде перемоги час,
І нам світитимуть великий Маркс і Гайне,
І вам — пророк Тарас.

Хай буря зла, мов звір,— її ми переборем.
В огні, в диму боїв одважно ми ідем
І з мудрим усміхом, як сивий Мойхер-Сфорім,—
Як Шварцман наш — з мечем.

Нас не зламать повік, бо ми не поодинці,
А попліч ідемо крізь темряву негод...
Не умирать, а жить, євреї, українці!
Нехай живе народ!

1942

To the Jewish People

Oh, people who gave the earth great geniuses,
People who carry from antiquity
A grand, honorable spirit despite wild slander—
    I bow down before you!

We ate the same bread, drank the same water.
We shared, like brothers, joy and sorrow,
And for this land—to keep it free—
    We will not hesitate to give our lives.

Once again, endless joy will spread,
From the bloody fight a time of victory
Will resume, and the great Marx and Heine
    Will shine for us, and for you—our prophet Taras.

Though the storm is furious as a beast—we'll overcome it.
Through the flames and smoke of battle
    we walk courageously,
With a witty smile, like the gray Moikher Sforim—
    Like our Shvartsman—with a sword.

No one will break us, because we're not divided,
We walk shoulder to shoulder through darkness,
    troubled times,
Not to die, but to live, the Jews, Ukrainians!
    Let the people live!

1942

Iurii Shcherbak (b. 1934) is a poet, fiction writer, screenwriter, epidemiologist, politician, diplomat, and environmental activist. Shcherbak worked as a researcher at the L. V. Hromashevs´kyi State Institute of Epidemiology and Infectious Diseases from 1958 to 1987, earning a PhD in 1965 and a doctor of medicine in 1983. He has published more than 100 articles and books in the field of science, and more than twenty volumes of poetry, prose, plays, and essays. His novel *Chornobyl´: dokumental´na povist´* was published in English in 1989 as *Chernobyl: A Documentary Story*. Shcherbak is the recipient of the Iurii Ianovs´kyi Literary Prize (1984), the Oleksandr Dovzhenko State Prize (1984), and the Antonovych Prize (2018). A former ambassador of Ukraine to the United States, Canada, and Israel, Shcherbak now lives in Kyiv.

Баскетбол

У Києві, на Сирці,
навпроти телевізійної вежі,
в олімпійському центрі
підготовки баскетболістів,
схожому на оранжерею,
походжають молоді велетні,
головою торкаючись кілець.
Тут пахне потом і м'ячами,
сонце весняне прикіпає,
хлопці у веселих червоних майках
м'яко скидають м'ячі у кошик,

а у вікно зазирають заздро
тіні тих, хто йшов тут
до Бабиного Яру
на розстріл,
усміхаються лагідно,
дивлячись на цих веселих гігантів,
і шепочуть:
перемагайте завжди, хлопці,
ніколи не знайте поразок,
тільки перемагайте,
онуки наші щасливі…

1984

Basketball

In Kyiv, in Syrets,
in front of the TV tower,
in the Olympic center
which looks like an orangery
where basketball players train,
young giants walk
touching rims with their heads.
It smells of sweat and basketballs,
the spring sun is firing,
guys in cheerful red t-shirts
swish shots through the net,

but peeping in the windows
are the shadows of those who
walked to Babyn Yar
to be executed,
they smile gently,
looking at these happy giants,
and whisper:
guys, you should always win,
never know loss,
only winning,
our happy grandsons…

1984

Vasyl′ Shvets′ (1918–93) was a poet and translator. He began publishing his work in the late 1930s and over the course of his life published several books including his collected works. During World War II, he served in the Red Army.

Бабин Яр

Не хвалися мені, не розказуй
і не плач. Я і так розумію,
як порвались легені від газу,
як навіки склепилися вії.

Уявляю: прикушені губи
в невимовній жадобі дихнути.
Сизий морок голодної згуби.
Невмолимість німої отрути.

Де ж повітря, що ніччю в кімнаті
з першим криком наповнило груди
і якого так дуже багато
над Подолом, над Києвом. Всюди!..

Духотою і смородом дише
чужоземного вечора хмара.
Плаче мати. Мовчання і тиша.
Ніч і стогін над Бабиним Яром.

Устають з-під землі наші діти,
закатовані, вдушені, вбиті,
недокохані нами і світом,
не научені твердо ходити.

Так приходить до них повноліття
в підземелля, трущоби і ями.
Так ітимуть вони крізь століття,
несучи на Німеччину плями.

Babyn Yar

Don't praise yourself, don't talk,
and don't weep. I already understand
how their lungs burst from the gas,
their eyelids were sealed forever.

I imagine bitten lips,
mute, yearning to breathe.
The blue darkness of starvation.
The unrelenting deaf poison.

But where did the air go
that filled lungs with the night
in the room at the first cry, so much screaming
over Podil, over all of Kyiv. Screaming everywhere!

The cloud of an alien evening
exhales its foul, airless breath.
A mother cries. Speechlessness, silence.
Night and moaning over Babyn Yar.

Our children, tortured, choked, killed,
not fully loved by us and the world,
not taught to walk steadily,
have risen from under the earth.

This is how they come of age
in the underground, the slums, and pits.
This is how they'll walk through centuries
carrying stains across Germany.

Плями помсти і гніву, і кривди
чим ти змиєш, убивце-народе?
Душогубку для світу відкрив ти,
і вина мимо тебе не пройде!

Не отруєним димом — петлею
чорне горло бандита обхватить
і вестиме в презирстві землею
з роду в рід і від хати до хати.

І задушить. І кине в безодню.
В лігво покидьок, гнилі і бруду.
Страшно суду? Не бійтесь! Сьогодні
ми бандитів караєм без суду!

Бабин яр — віковічна могила,
як дитинство, невинна і світла.
Скільки, скільки ти душ загубила,
Душогубко — Німеччино підла?!

3. III. 1944

The stains of vengeance and rage,
How will you scrub them out, you nation of killers?
You invented the gas van,
and this guilt won't pass you by!

Not poisonous gas—a rope will
collar the criminal's black throat
as he's dragged around the earth
from generation to generation, house to house.

You'll choke and be thrown into the abyss.
Into a den of scum, rot, and filth.
Are you afraid of judgment? Don't be! Today
we punish criminals without trial!

Babyn Yar is an eternal grave,
like childhood, sinless and bright.
How many, how many souls have you killed,
you, the soul-killer, vile Germany?!

March 3, 1944

Volodymyr Sosiura (1898–1965) was a poet and writer. He was very productive during his lifetime and published several dozen poetry collections. In 1942–44, Sosiura was a war correspondent. His collected works have been published in three-volume editions (1929–30 and 1957–58) and in a ten-volume edition (1970–72). The autobiographical novel *Tretia rota* (The third company) appeared posthumously in the time of perestroika in 1988. In 1948, Sosiura was awarded the highest literary award, the Stalin Prize.

Єврейському народові

Ти йшов крізь ніч, крізь біль, віками гнаний.
крізь дим кострів, погромів дикий дим.
Між гострих скель шукав ти Ханаану,
в пісках пустинь, йдучи шляхом важким.

Ти йшов віки крізь довгу ніч залізну,
крізь сльози й кров, і от дійшов мети:
в країні Рад знайшов свою вітчизну,
між вільних нас розквітнув вільно ти.

З тобою дім ми світлий збудували,
щоб жить у нім, на радість поколінь.
Та час прийшов у гуркоті металу,
і з заходу упала грізна тінь.

І знову зойк, і стогони, й прокльони,
погромів дим і шибениць хрести.
Народи йдуть на бій многоколонно,
і з ними йдеш на бій безстрашно ти.

Ми встали всі у вихорі негоди,
злились в одно, ллючи за щастя кров,
і ненависть твоя, оновлений народе,
є наша ненависть, як і твоя любов.

Ми заженем разом в безодню звіра,
брунатних орд розвієм чорний прах,
бо рідний край ми любимо без міри,
бо Сталін нас вперед веде в боях.

To the Jewish People

You walked all night in pain, persecuted through centuries.
Through the smoke of fires, the wild smoke of pogroms.
Along cliffsides you looked for Canaan,
In deserts, always walking a difficult path.

You walked centuries through a long steel night,
through tears and blood, and finally you reached the goal:
in the country of the Soviets you found your homeland,
among us, the free, you flourished.

Together we built a bright home
to live in, for the joy of generations.
But the time arrived roaring with metal,
and a menacing shadow cast from the West.

And again howl, groan, and curse,
the smoke of pogroms and the crosses of gallows.
The nations go into battle in many columns,
and with them you walk fearlessly.

Together we weathered the whirlwind,
merged into one, pouring blood for happiness,
and your hatred, you rejuvenated people,
is our hatred, as well as your love.

We'll drive the beast together into the abyss,
we'll scatter the black ashes of brownshirt hordes,
because we love our native land beyond measure,
because Stalin is leading us forward into battle.

Наш світлий дім сіятиме над світом,
іще ясніш він встане у блакить.
бо зір Кремля нікому не згасити,
і серця бій народів не спинить.

1942

Our bright home will shine across the world,
rise even more visibly into the sky.
Because the eyes of the Kremlin can't be closed,
and no one can stop the beating heart of our nations.

1942

Бабин Яр

Сюди водили їх і ставили підряд,
І чужоземна гавкала команда...
Розстрілювали їх «во славу фатерлянда»,
І падали вони, сестра і друг, і брат,

і падали вони: коханий і дружина,
і мати, й дитинча, бабуся й дід сумний,
без крику, мовчки всі... Свята їх смерть невинна,
як пам'ятник в віках, безсмертний, краю мій!

Їх тисячі лягло у Бабин Яр глибокий,
і трамбували їх у тім яру кати...
Топтали їх тіла... Ридали хмари: «доки?»...
Схиляли злякані голівоньки цвіти,

і сльози капали з леліток їх криваві,
На землю стерзану, де йшли в останній раз,
Безсмертні смертники... І шепотіли трави:
«Вони пішли на смерть, бо так любили нас,

упали, як один, вони у тьму могили,
розстрілювали їх сліпі потвори мли,
за те, що небо це і землю цю любили,
що вірними тобі, Україно, були!»...

Щоб злочини свій страшний од кари заховати,
руками бранців їх знов витягли на світ
і склали з трупів їх високії кагати
і віддали вогню... Вітчизни рідний цвіт,

Babyn Yar

They were marched here and lined up,
and an order was barked in a foreign language...
They were machine-gunned for the "glory of the Vaterland,"
and they fell down, sister and friend and brother,

and they fell down: husband and wife,
mother and child, grandmother and grandfather,
without screaming, silently... Their death was righteous,
a monument for centuries, immortal, my country!

Thousands buried in deep Babyn Yar,
and the executioners packed them down in that ravine...
Trampled their bodies... The clouds cried: "How long?"...
The flowers bowed their terrified heads,

and bloody tears dripped from the petals
to the earth where they walked for the last time,
immortals destined for death... And the grass whispered:
"They walked toward death because they loved us,

they fell down, as one, into the darkness of the grave,
they were gunned down by the blind monsters of fog,
because they loved this sky and earth,
because they were faithful to you, Ukraine!"...

To cover the cruel crimes from prosecution,
they were unearthed by prisoners' hands
and tall heaps of their corpses rose
and were burnt... The native blossom of the motherland,

як тяжко ти горів, як линув дим од тебе,
на Куренівку, вдаль, і виснув над Дніпром,
і припадав до трав, і підіймавсь до неба,
як грізний велетень з нахмуреним чолом...

Він линув все на схід, туди, де бою згуки
все ближче до Дніпра зітхали і гули,
він простягав братам криваві й довгі руки,
до помсти кликав їх... і йшли брати, і йшли,

по трупах ворогів, а дим стелився низько,
їм припадав до рук і плечі цілував,
і повертався назад, крізь залпів гострі блиски,
і в небі звивами, неначе малював:

«Вони вже близько, йдуть... Катам за наші муки
вони відплатять так, що і не снилось їм!»
І простягав в громах на захід гнівні руки,
з прокляттям на вустах од жертв невинних дим...

і сталось так, брати, як марили ми з вами,
він знову вільний, наш, золотоверхий рай,
наш Київ дорогий!.. Я зрошую сльозами
холодні ті стежки, де вів вас ворог злий,

брати мої святі і сестри карооки!..
за вас ми вже мстимось і смерті смерть несем...
Вони вас кинули у Бабин Яр глибокий,
А ми в безодню їх до одного зметем...

how you burnt in pain, how your smoke drifted toward
Kurenivka, further on, and hung above the Dnipro,
and crouched in the grass, and ascended to the sky,
like a menacing giant with a furrowed forehead...

He kept echoing eastward, where the sounds of a fight
rumbled and sighed closer to the Dnipro,
he stretched his arms covered in blood to his brothers,
urged them to avenge... and our brothers kept coming

over the corpses of our enemies, the smoke descended low,
pressed their hands and kissed their shoulders,
and went back, through the sharp brightness of artillery
and zigzagging in the sky as if sketching:

"They're so close, they're coming... They'll avenge
our anguish in a way we couldn't have dreamt of!"
And stretched, in thunder, wrathful hands westward,
with curses on their lips, smoke from innocent victims...

And it happened, my brothers, as we'd imagined,
it's free again, our golden-domed paradise,
our dear Kyiv!... I irrigate with my tears
those cold trails, where the evil enemy led you,

my holy brothers and browned-eyed sisters!...
We're already avenging you, carrying death to death...
They threw you into deep Babyn Yar,
and we'll sweep them all into an abyss...

Од страдників вони святий лишили попіл,
Розвіяний в вітрах, він чорними слізьми
Вкраїну оросив і на поля Європи
рясним дощем упав, як знак, що скоро тьми

не буде вже ніде, що кара невблаганно
на голови катів обрушує свій меч,
і меч тримають той, в бою разом із нами
замучені брати. Вже слуха крик утеч

мій край, де рідна кров з могил крізь землю била,
де смерті таборів лишилися дроти,
й руїни наших міст, і сел сумні могили,
і тіні од людей, і зірвані мости...

Ми знайдемо усіх, хто кров точив дитячу,
Хто бабиних ярів лишив страшні ряди,
де й досі ще вітри над нами в тузі плачуть,
і плач той у віках не змовкне назавжди.

Сюди водили їх... В сльозах моє обличчя...
А Бабин Яр мовчить, тривоги повний вщерть,
і попіл страдників у серці стука й кличе
нас, іменем життя, попрати смертю смерть!

1943

From martyrs, they left holy ashes,
dissipated on the wind, watered
Ukraine with black tears and fell on the fields
of Europe, heavy rain, a sign that soon there'd be

no darkness anywhere, that punishment relentlessly
points its sword at the heads of executioners,
and that sword is wielded by brothers killed
in action. My native land listens to the cries

of flight, where the blood of relatives fountains
from the earth,
where barbed wire is what's left of death camps,
and the ruins of our cities, and sad graves in villages,
and shadows of people, and bombed bridges...

We'll find everyone who spilled the blood of children,
who left the horrendous rows of corpses in ravines,
where still the wind cries above us out of sorrow
and that cry won't stop through the centuries.

They were brought here... My face is covered in tears...
And Babyn Yar remains silent, full of dread,
and the ashes of martyrs beat in our hearts and call us
in the name of life, wash death with death!

1943

Marta Tarnawsky (1930–2021) was a poet, translator, bibliographer, essayist, reviewer, journalist, and community activist. Born in Ukraine, she came to the United States in 1949. She published four collections of Ukrainian poetry: *Khvaliu iliuziu* (I praise illusion, 1972), *Zemletrus* (Earthquake, 1981), *Samotnie mistse pid sontsem* (A solitary place under the sun, 1991), and *Tykhi rozmovy z vichnistiu* (Quiet conversations with eternity, 1999). She also published collections of essays, two personal bibliographies, and a multi-volume major bibliography: *Ukrainian Literature in English*. As an essayist, reviewer, critic, and bibliographer, she was the author of numerous articles and essays in various publications. She published 816 items, of which seventeen were separate books or pamphlets.

В житті моєму теж був Бабин Яр

В житті моєму теж був Бабин Яр:

Ішли по вісім вулицею міста —
діди, чоловіки, жінки і діти —
і понад ними нісся дивний гул:
мов стогін сотні скарг, немов скигління,
мов здавлений у горлі дикий плач.

Попереду сивоволосий муж —
високий, у розстебнутій сорочці,
з піднятою угору головою —
це наш знайомий, Ґольдберґ, наш сусід.
Він був не раббі — він був тільки лікар,
він філософію любив і був музика.
(Звичайно він життя лиш рятував,
та довелося рятувати гідність).

Довкола ліс баґнетів на рушницях —
конвой із педантичних молодців.
Шоломи світять в сонці, мов на свято,
і блиск іде від чищених чобіт.
Чи хлопці ці також читали Ґете
і слухали «Тангойзера» й «Ізольду»?
Чи й серед них — філософи й музики?

Мені дванадцять років. Від вікна
мене насилу відтягає мати.
Вона стискає у зубах п'ястук
і кров із пальців маже їй обличчя.
Мене кладуть у ліжко. Я в гарячці.
Мені ввижається в стіні розбитий череп.

In my life too there was a Babyn Yar

In my life too there was a Babyn Yar:

Marched eight at a time down the city's streets—
men, women, old people, and children—
and above them a strange sound drifted:
the groan of a hundred complaints, a howling,
a wild scream stifled in the throat.

In front, a gray-haired man—
tall, shirt unbuttoned,
his head raised—
this was our neighbor, Goldberg, our doctor.
He wasn't a rabbi—he was just a doctor,
he loved philosophy, was a musician.
(Usually, he was simply saving lives,
but now he had to save his dignity.)

Surrounded by a forest of bayonets,
a convoy of fastidious young men.
Helmets gleam in the sun as if it's a holiday,
polished boots flash and shine.
Have these boys ever read Goethe
and listened to Tannhäuser and Isolda?
Any philosophers or musicians among them?

I'm twelve. My mother grabs me,
pulls me away from the window.
She bites her fist, bloody
fingers smear her face.
They put me to bed. I have a fever.
I have a vision of a broken skull on a wall.

Немає тільки батька. Він — в стодолі,
в чужім селі, заритий в сіно, скрився
перечекати ніч, що вдень настала.
Та він — не сам. Із ним сусід наш, Ґольдберґ,
син лікаря, філософа й музики.

1972

My father's away. He's in a barn,
in a different village, covered in hay, he hid
to wait through a night that had arrived during the day.
But he's not alone. With him is our neighbor, Goldberg,
the son of the doctor, philosopher, and musician.

1972

Pavlo Tychyna (1891–1967) was arguably the greatest Ukrainian poet of the twentieth century. His early collections *Soniachni klarnety* (Clarinets of the sun; 1918), *Pluh* (The plow; 1920), *Zamist´ sonetiv i oktav* (Instead of sonnets and octaves; 1920), *Viter z Ukraïny* (The wind from Ukraine; 1924) are often considered the pinnacle of his creativity. His later collections of poetry include *Chernihiv* (1931) and *Partiia vede* (The party leads; 1933). He continued to write and publish considerably during and after World War II. His collected works in twelve volumes appeared in the 1980s. A collection of his early poetry was published in English translation in 2017 under the title *Pavlo Tychyna: The Complete Early Poetry Collections*.

Єврейському народові

Народ єврейський! Славний! Не втішать
тебе я хочу. Кожен хай тут слуха:
в цей час, коли синам твоїм вмирать
прийшлося від фашистського обуха,—
я хочу силу, силу оспівать —
безсмертну, вічну силу твого духа!

Вона родилась ще давно — тоді,
як був ти нерозсіяним і цілим.
Буяли в тобі сили молоді!
І розцвітав цвітастий шлях, як килим...
Та ось підкрався ворог — і в біді
ти голубом забився сизокрилим.

Ах, голуб, голуб!.. Образ він душі
твоєї був колись...Але як стався
той злам, коли і ниву й спориші
тобі стоптали й ти не покорявся
врагу, а кинув поклик «сокруши!» —
то образ голуба на сокола змінявся.

О, скільки раз в середньовіччі ти
скорятись не хотів ні королеві,
ні герцогам! Й було не страшно йти,
коли звучали голоси сталеві
і Ібн Габірола з темноти,
і Езри, й Іуди — мужнього Галеві!

А в дев'ятнадцятий суворий вік —
ой, скільки від царів ти настраждався!
«Еврей? — сміялись: — це ж не чоловік

To the Jewish People

Glorious Jewish people! I'm not here
to console you. Listen, everyone:
while your sons are bludgeoned
with the dull back of a fascist axe—
I want to sing your strength—
the eternal strength of your spirit!

It was born a long time ago—when
you were united, not dispersed.
Young strength flowered inside you!
And the blooming path rolled out like a carpet...
But an enemy crept up—and in this turmoil
you sheltered like a blue-winged dove.

Oh, dove, dove!... It was once an image
of your soul... But when this tumult
came, when your crops and grasslands
were trampled over, you didn't surrender
but shouted out "Attack!"—
and the pigeon became a falcon.

How many times through the Middle Ages
did you refuse to surrender to queens
or dukes! And you weren't afraid to march
when the iron voices of Solomon ibn Gabirol,
of Ezra, and courageous Judah Halevi resounded!

And in the stern nineteenth century—
how much you suffered under the tsars!
"A Jew?" they laughed. "A Jew is not a man,

і не людина». І в колючках слався
твій шлях,—і шлях, здавалось, вже заник...
Аж тут Шолом-Алейхем засміявся!..

Цей сміх, мов нерозгризений горіх,
все на царів котивсь, котивсь... Лиш згодом,
як розкотився він по стежках всіх
далеко й опинився між народом,—
царі тривогу вдарили. Та тих
не вбить, в яких життя кипить підсподом...

Життя усіх нас красно розцвіло
лише в безсмертнім Жовтні. Вічно слався
свободи час, коли тирана зло
повержено! Й еврей тоді назвався
бійцем. За волю скільки їх лягло! —
між них і Ошер Шварцман красувався...

Красується ж і зараз він. Слова
його нам: «Югенд, югенд» — так потрібні!
О молодість! Ти молодість нова
єврейського народу! Непохибні
шляхи твої тепер. Душа жива
за правду дзвонить людям в дзвони срібні...

Але ж на Заході! — твої брати
і сестри в кігтях звіра-людоїда
ще тяжко мучаться. О, де знайти
тих слів, щоб висловить: яка огида
проймає нас до нього! Не гніти,
проклятий! Правда встане вогневида!

not a human." Your path drove through thorns—
until it nearly disappeared. But suddenly
Sholom Aleichem burst out laughing!

This laughter, like an uncracked nut,
kept rolling and rolling towards the tsars... Finally,
when it rolled across all the roads
and arrived among the people—
the tsars sounded the alarm. But people
so full of life aren't easy to kill...

Our lives truly blossomed
during the October Revolution. Eternal glory
to that time of freedom, when tyranny
was overthrown. Then, a Jew called himself
a warrior. So many died for freedom! —
among them, Osher Shvartsman shone.

He's still shining. "Jugend, jugend,"
we need his words now as ever.
O, youth! You are the new youth
of the Jewish people! Your path
is unobstructed. Your vibrant soul
rings the silver bell of truth to everyone.

But in the West!—your brothers
and sisters are in the claws of a cannibal,
still in agony. O, where do I find
the words to express how we
loathe him! Stop your tyranny and be
damned! The truth will flash like fire!

Вона поборе! Правда вже встає!
І там, де греки, серби і хорвати,
виковується гнів. Вже виграє
сурма для помсти. Доки ж, доки ждати?
Чи мо хай душогуб усіх уб'є?—
Повстанцям час до битви вирушати.

Й повстанці йдуть, в стратегії своїй
то появляються, то в ліс зникають…
Кипи, наш гнів, грозою пломеній
за дике гетто у Європі! Знають
хай німчики, що є відплата:—Стій!
По всьому світу грози наростають…

І ми—під переблиски блискавиць,
під грім тих гроз народів—тяжкість грузу
з євреїв скинемо. Доволі ниць
лежати їм! Доволі мук і глузу
дурного Гітлера! Залізна міць
підниметься з Радянського Союзу!

Ми чуєм із Європи плач: Рахіль
за дітьми за своїми тужить,—мати
вбивається… Ах, сльози ці і біль
в віках обвинуваченням звучати
проти німоти будуть! Їй як сіль
в очах еврей. Ну, що на це сказати?

Народ єврейський! Славний! Не втішать
тебе я хочу. Кожен хай тут слуха:
В цей час, коли синам твоїм вмирать

It will triumph! The truth has begun rising!
And where Greeks, Serbs, and Croats are,
its wrath is being forged. The trumpet is
calling for vengeance. How long do we wait?
Or else let the murderer kill everyone?—
It's time for insurgents to fight back.

And the insurgents cunningly slip out of
the woods or disappear into them...
Let our wrath boil, ignite like a thunderstorm,
the unthinkable ghettos in Europe! Let the Germans
know there will be vengeance: —Halt!
Across the whole world, the thunderstorms increase.

And we—under the flash of lightning,
the thunder of the people—will release the weight
burdening the Jews, dragging them
flat to the ground. Enough of the torture,
the mockery, from Hitler! The iron might
of the Soviet Union will rise!

We hear the keening from Europe: Rakhil
mourning for her children, a mother's
lament... O, these tears and pain
will resound through centuries, an accusation
against their silence! For them, a Jew is
like salt in the eye. Well, what can I say?

Glorious Jewish people! I'm not here
to console you. Listen, everyone:
while your sons are bludgeoned

прийшлося від фашистського обуха,—
я хочу силу, силу оспівать, —
безсмертну, вічну силу твого духа.

15-16 вересня 1942

with the dull back of a fascist axe—
I want to sing your strength—
the eternal strength of your spirit!

September 15–16, 1942

„Кам'минь"

727, 1, 3

Annotations

Arkadii Anin, "Monologue of a Monument Never Built" (p. 47).

Ukrainian-language poem reprinted from Arkadii Anin, *Dotyk* (Kyiv, 1997), 102.

The date of this poem is based on its inclusion in the 1997 Anin collection. The poem is part of a longer cycle entitled "Babyn Yar."

Arkadii Anin, "Monologue of the Monument" (p. 49).

Ukrainian-language poem reprinted from Arkadii Anin, *Dotyk* (Kyiv, 1997), 103.

The date of this poem is based on its inclusion in the 1997 Anin collection. The poem is part of a longer cycle entitled "Babyn Yar."

Mykola Bazhan, "Ravine" (p. 53).

Ukrainian-language poem reprinted from Mykola Bazhan, *V dni viiny* (Kyiv: Viis´kove vydavnytstvo narodnoho komisariatu oborony, 1945), 63–65.

Written in 1943, the poem was published in the collection as part four of the cycle called "Kyivs´ki etiudy" (The Kyiv etudes), which consists of seven parts and may be the poet's first artistic response to the city immediately after it was retaken by the Red Army in 1943.

This poem was published, for the first time, as "The Ravine" in an English translation by Peter Tempest in the journal *Ukrainian Canadian* (January 1977): 37. This translation, most likely produced from a Russian translation, later appeared online in a revised and edited version by Boris Dralyuk (Mykola Bazhan, *Babi Yar: The Source and Translations*, http://polyhymnion.org/lit/bazhan/). There are two other English versions of the poem available: Roman Turovsky's translation and Amelia Glaser's translation, both published in *Odessa Review* 5 (October/November 2016): 39, https://issuu.com/theodessareview/docs/_5issue.

For more information in English on Mykola Bazhan and Babyn Yar see Lev Fridman, "In Search of Mykola Bazhan's Legacy on The Eve of Babyn Yar Commemorations," *Odessa Review* 5 (October/November 2016): 34–45, https://issuu.com/theodessareview/docs/_5issue.

How beyond the crowns of Kyryliv's buildings: for Kyryliv, see Geographical Locations.

Valeriia Bohuslavs´ka, "For Marianna Kiyanovska—in Response to Her Book *The Voices of Babyn Yar*" (p. 61).

Ukrainian-language poem reprinted from Valeriia Bohuslavs´ka, *Zemlia abetkovana: riznomanitni virshi* (Kyiv: Vydavnychyi dim "Buraho," 2018), 95. The dating of the poem is based on my communication with the author.

Poems from Marianna Kiyanovska's collection *Babyn Iar. Holosamy* (The Voices of Babyn Yar) are available in this volume.

Leonid Cherevatenko, "Michelangelo" (p. 65).

Ukrainian-language poem reprinted from Leonid Cherevatenko, *Vidkrytyi zvuk* (Kyiv: Radians´kyi pys´mennyk, 1982), 39.

The date of the poem is based on the information available in the anthology: Iurii Kaplan, ed., *Vidlunnia Babynoho Iaru* (Kyiv, 2006), 137.

Leonid Cherevatenko, "1941: The Jewish Question" (p. 71).
Ukrainian-language poem reprinted from Leonid Cherevatenko, *Zakliate zalizo* (Kyiv: Dukh i litera, 2012), 130–32. The date of the poem is based on my communication with Valeriia Bohuslavs´ka.

Leonid Cherevatenko, "The Gorgon Medusa" (p. 67).
Ukrainian-language poem reprinted from Leonid Cherevatenko, *Zakliate zalizo* (Kyiv: Dukh i litera, 2012), 133. The date of the poem is based on my communication with Valeriia Bohuslavs´ka.

Borys Dabo-Nikolaiev, "Tested by Babyn Yar" (p. 81).
Ukrainian-language poem reprinted from Borys Dabo-Nikolaiev, , *Kyievu—Vsesvitovi mistu* (Kyiv: Zadruha, 2001), 29. The date of the poem is derived from information received from the poet.
The poet's mother (Ol´ha Nikolaieva-Kochmarzhyns´ka) helped Father Oleksii Hlaholiev (later, a member of the Righteous Among the Nations) obtain documents to legalize the Jews who had survived Babyn Yar. On September 29, 1941, she witnessed the Jews walking along Taras Shevchenko Boulevard towards Halyts´ka Square. The poem "Tested by Tragedy" reflects her impressions and emotions. (This note was given to the editor by the poet.)
from Halyts´ka square: for Halyts´ka Square, see Glossary.

Ivan Drach, "[On June 22, 1966, at five in the afternoon]" (p. 85).

Ukrainian-language poem reprinted from Ivan Drach, *Do dzherel* (Kyiv: Dnipro, 1972), 109. The date of the poem is based on its initial publication in a journal.

The poem first appeared in the literary journal *Dnipro*, no. 10 (1966): 68, as part of a larger submission. The following year, the poem was featured in the collection *Poeziï* (Kyiv: Molod´, 1967), 160. The same year it was also reprinted in the Slovak Ukrainian-language journal *Duklia* no. 6 (1967): 35. A few years later, the poem was collected in the volume *Do dzherel* (Kyiv: Dnipro, 1972), 109.

An English translation of this poem by Daniel Halpern, entitled "Babi Yar," appeared in the collection of poems by Ivan Drach edited by Stanley Kunitz and translated by American poets: Ivan Drach, *Orchard Lamps* (New York: Sheep Meadow, 1978), 8.

Ivan Drach, "A Kyiv Legend" (p. 87).

Ukrainian-language poem reprinted from Ivan Drach, *Kyïvs´ke nebo* (Kyiv: Molod´, 1976), 7–8. The date of the poem is based on its publication in the poet's collection.

Today our path goes across the Dnipro: for the Dnipro, see Glossary.

The 1st Ukrainian Front: The 1st Ukrainian Front was a group-level formation of the Soviet army that existed from 1943 to 1945. From 1944 to 1945, the Front was commanded by Nikolai Vatutin, Georgii Zhukov, and Ivan Konev during battles in Ukraine, Poland, Germany and Czechoslovakia. The Front's last actions were part of the Prague Offensive in May 1945.

I'm Kyi, a porter working this river... Sail to the Cossack island, Shchek... You, brother Khoryv, break through... This is Lybid´, our sister: Kyi, Shchek, Khoryv and their sister Lybid´ are three legendary brothers and a sister who founded the medieval city of Kyiv according to the *Primary Chronicle,* which is traditionally believed to have been written by the monk Nestor and finished in 1113. In 1982, Kyi, Shchek, Khoryv and Lybid´ were depicted on an ancient riverboat in a sculpture created by Vasyl´ Borodai and installed in one of the parks in Kyiv. This sculpture became iconic for the city.

Near the Lavra a German opens cannon-jaws: for Lavra, see Glossary.

Vatutin drinks holy water from the Dnipro: Nikolai Vatutin (1901–44) was a Soviet Army General of the Soviet Union who led the 1st Ukrainian Front during World War II. General Nikolai Vatutin spoke at the Babyn Yar site after the Red Army recaptured the city: "Each of you knows about the atrocities of the Nazi monsters in Kyiv. In 1941 alone the vile Fascist animals exterminated over 85,000 peaceful residents of Kyiv—women, old people, children. The blood in our veins freezes as we discover the terrible picture of the Fascist cannibals' terrible crime in Babyn Yar" (Serhy Yekelchyk, *Stalin's Children: Everyday Politics in the Wake of Total War* [New York: Oxford University Press, 2014], 13).

Hryhorii Fal´kovych, "[From that horrible time]" (p. 93).

Ukrainian-language poem reprinted from the author's manuscript sent to the editor. The date of the poem is based on information received from the author.

This poem appeared earlier in the poet's collection *Spoviduius´, use beru na sebe...* [I confess; I accept it all...] (Kyiv: Ukraïns´kyi pys´mennyk, 1994),10–11, and was part of the cycle "Babyn Yar."

Hryhorii Fal´kovych, "[Indian Summer in Babyn Yar]" (p. 95).

Ukrainian-language poem reprinted from the author's manuscript sent to the editor. The date of the poem is based on information received from the author.

This poem appeared earlier in the poet's collection *Spoviduius´, use beru na sebe...* [I confess; I accept it all...] (Kyiv: Ukraïns´kyi

pys´mennyk, 1994), 10–11, in a different version, and was part of a longer cycle entitled "Babyn Yar."
Indian summer in Babyn Yar: in Ukrainian, "babyne lito" means Indian summer.

Hryhorii Fal´kovych, "[On the Eve of Holy Sabbath]" (p. 97).
Ukrainian-language poem reprinted from the author's manuscript sent to the editor. The date of the poem is based on information received from the author.
This poem appeared earlier in the poet's collection *Spoviduius´, use beru na sebe...* [I confess; I accept it all...] (Kyiv: Ukraïns´kyi pys´mennyk, 1994), 11, and was part of a cycle entitled "Babyn Iar."

Moisei Fishbein, "Ravine" (p. 101).
Ukrainian-language poem reprinted from Moisei Fishbein, *Rannii rai* (Kyiv: Fakt, 2006), 104–5. Initially, the poem appeared in: Moisei Fishbein, *Zbirka bez nazvy* (Suchanist´, 1984), 34–35.

Iakiv Hal´perin [pseudonym Mykola Pervach], "Laughter" (p. 107).
Ukrainian text reprinted from Mykola Pervach [Iakiv Hal´perin], "Smikh," *Litavry*, no. 3 (30 November 1941), 2.
The poem was later republished in a slightly different version in an anthology edited by Ritalii Zaslavskii under the Russian title *Piatnadtsat´ poetov—piatnadtsat´ sudeb* (Kyiv: Zhurnal "Raduga," 2002), 87–88.
Hal´perin, a Kyiv-born Jew, remained in Kyiv during the Nazi occupation. With help from his Ukrainian friends, he acquired forged identification documents with a Ukrainian name and published his work, under the pseudonym Mykola Pervach, in the Nazi-controlled Kyiv-based literary journal *Litavry* and Prague-based journal *Proboiem*. After two years in Kyiv, Hal´perin was captured and, most likely, executed by the Nazis

in 1943. His 1941 poem, the journalist Olena Bilozers´ka argued, is probably one of the first, if not the first, poem on Babyn Yar composed in Ukrainian (Olena Bilozers´ka, "Ohydnyi renehat chy patriot Ukraïny?" *Ukrainskie itogi* [October 2007], https://bilozerska.livejournal.com/21067.html).

For more information on this poem as well as its author, see: Naum Korzhavin, "V soblaznakh krovavoi epokhi," *Novyi mir*, 1992, no. 8, 130–93; I. Lazitskaia, "...Pravo na nastoiashchuiu zhizn´...," *Raduga*, 2006, no. 12, 147–69; Mark Berdichevskii, "Kiev sorok piatogo goda. Pamiati Iakova Gal´perina. Stikhi," *Kontinent* 136 (2008), https://magazines.gorky.media/continent/2008/136/kiev-sorok-pyatogo-goda.html; Oleksandr Kucheruk, "Mykola Pervach: '... i vy pochuiete shche znovu i znovu prorochu movu," *Orhanizatsiia ukraïns´kykh natsionalistiv*, October 10, 2016, http://kmoun.info/2016/10/10/oleksandr-kucheruk-mikola-pervach-i-vi-pochuyete-shhe-znovu-i-znovu-poetovu-prorochu-movu/.

Sava Holovanivs´kyi, "Melnyk Street" (p. 113).

Ukrainian-language poem reprinted from Sava Holovanivs´kyi, *Synii ptakh: poeziï* (Kyiv: Radians´kyi pys´mennyk, 1980), 49–51. The date of the poem is noted in the poetry collection.

Melnyk Street: see Glossary.

Sava Holovanivs´kyi penned another poem related to Babyn Yar entitled "Avraam" (Abraham). Even though some scholars have mentioned the poem in their studies, the text remains undiscovered. I assume the poem was written and published during the Second World War or shortly thereafter and printed in one of the newspapers or journals. Later, the poem became evidence used against the poet during the writers' convention which coincided with the anti-Semitic campaigns of 1948–49. Holovanivs´kyi was condemned for depicting Ukrainians and Russians as bystanders who watched passively as a Jew was marched by the Nazis to the ravine: "Holovanivs´kyi is the author of a nationalistic poem, openly inimical towards the Soviet people. In this poem, Holovanivs´kyi makes a terrible and never-before-seen slander towards the Soviet people and he lies through his teeth by speaking as if the Soviet people—Russians and Ukrainians—apathetically looked away from an old Jewish man called Avraam whom the Germans marched for execution through the streets of Kyiv" (L. Dmiterko [Liubomyr Dmyterko], "Sostoianie i zadachi teatral´noi i literaturnoi kritiki na Ukraine," *Literaturnaia gazeta* 20 [9 March 1949], 2).

Holovanivs´kyi also worked on *The Black Book of Soviet Jewry* edited by Ilya Ehrenburg and Vasilii Grossman, but in the end his pieces did not appear in their book. His contributions—"Gibel´ evreev Khar´kova. Vospominaniia Niny Mogilevskoi, zheny rabochego-avtogenshchika" and "Kazn´ v Mariupole. Pis´mo Samuila Aronovicha Belousa"—were included in the following volume: *Neizvesnaia "Chernaia kniga"*, ed. Il´ia Al´tman (Moscow: AST; Corpus, 2015), 92–95, 109–112.

Denys Holubyts´kyi, "[The stones of my brothers and the sky of my sisters]" (p. 119).

Ukrainian-language poem reprinted from Denys Holubyts´kyi, "Ievreis´kyi tsykl," *Ukraïns´ka literaturna hazeta* (October 15, 2020). https://litgazeta.com.ua/poetry/denys-holubytskyj-ievrejskyj-tsykl/.

On the street of angels: during the Soviet times, Liuteranska (Lutheran) Street was Engels Street. In German, "engel" means "angel."

Maybe Esther: an allusion to the novel by Ukrainian-born German-language writer Katja Petrowskaja *Maybe Esther: A Family Story*. An English translation, by Shelley Frisch, was published in 2018.

Crawl, Liuteranska street, crawl: see Glossary.

And again the street runs down into the embraces of Khreshchatyk: see Glossary.

Oleksa Iushchenko, "Babyn Yar" (p. 125).

Ukrainian-language poem reprinted from Oleksa Iushchenko, *Vybrane* (Kyiv: Dnipro, 1977), 40–41. The date of the poem is based on information mentioned in: Iurii Kaplan, ed. *Vidlunnia Babynoho Iaru* (2006).

And Luk'ianivka is shaking as though: see Glossary.

Igor Kaczurowskyj, "To Marta Tarnawsky" (p. 131).

Ukrainian-language poem reprinted from Ihor Kachurovs′kyi, *Liryka*, ed. Volodymyr Bazylevs′kyi and Olena O'Lir (Lviv: Astroliabiia, 2013), 211–12. The poem was also featured in the poet's collection *Svichada vichnosty* (Munich: Instytut literatury im. M. Oresta, 1990), 98. Initially, the poem appeared, in a slightly different form, under the title of "Marti Tarnavs′kii" in: *Suchasnist′*, no. 9 (1983): 22.

Abram Katsnel′son, "In Babyn Yar" (p. 135).

Ukrainian-language poem reprinted from Abram Katsnel′son, *Liryka* (Kyiv: Astarta, 2002), 237.

Abram Katsnel′son, "Grandson's Monologue" (p. 137).

Ukrainian-language poem reprinted from Abram Katsnel′son, *Liryka* (Kyiv: Astarta, 2002), 237–38.

Abram Katsnel′son, "Kyiv. September 29. Babyn Yar" (p. 139).

Ukrainian-language poem reprinted from Abram Katsnel′son, *Liryka* (Kyiv: Astarta, 2002), 238.

Marianna Kiyanovska, "[i would die on this street or on the one around the corner]" (p. 143).

Ukrainian-language poem reprinted from Marianna Kiianovs´ka, *Babyn Iar. Holosamy* (Kyiv: Dukh i litera, 2017), 11.

Marianna Kiyanovska, "[i even managed to grow during the war]" (p. 145).

Ukrainian-language poem reprinted from Marianna Kiianovs´ka, *Babyn Iar. Holosamy* (Kyiv: Dukh i litera, 2017), 30.

Marianna Kiyanovska, "[i will say it anyway i will accept it anyway]" (p. 147).

Ukrainian-language poem reprinted from Marianna Kiianovs´ka, *Babyn Iar. Holosamy* (Kyiv: Dukh i litera, 2017), 41.

i was on the dnipro yesterday actually not on the dnipro: for Dnipro, see Glossary.

Marianna Kiyanovska, "[these streets are already ruins maybe not all but already]," (p. 149).

Ukrainian-language poem reprinted from Marianna Kiianovs´ka, *Babyn Iar. Holosamy* (Kyiv: Dukh i litera, 2017), 55.

Marianna Kiyanovska, "[i've been getting together a collection for the last three weeks]" (p. 151).

Ukrainian-language poem reprinted from Marianna Kiianovs´ka, *Babyn Iar. Holosamy* (Kyiv: Dukh i litera, 2017), 62.

Marianna Kiyanovska, "[here is the ravine where hans does his shooting]" (p. 155).

Ukrainian-language poem reprinted from Marianna Kiianovs´ka, *Babyn Iar. Holosamy* (Kyiv: Dukh i litera, 2017), 95.

Dmytro Pavlychko, "[On the edge of Babyn Yar]" (p. 161).
Ukrainian-language poem reprinted from Dmytro Pavlychko, *Vybrani tvory* (Kyiv: Dnipro, 1979), 2:135. The date of the poem is based on the information from this edition.

Dmytro Pavlychko, "[Walking near Babyn Yar]" (p. 159).
Ukrainian-language poem reprinted from Dmytro Pavlychko, *Vybrani tvory* (Kyiv: Dnipro, 1979), 2:136. The date of the poem is based on information from this edition.

Dmytro Pavlychko, "Requiem. Babyn Yar" (p. 163).
Ukrainian-language poem reprinted from Dmytro Pavlychko, "Rekviiem. Babyn Iar," *Vechirnii Kyïv* 95 (21 May 1991).
In the 1991 *Vechirnii Kyïv* publication, the poem contains a lengthy introduction penned by Dmytro Pavlychko, in which the poet underlined the significance of the Babyn Yar tragedy. He compares it with the Chernobyl catastrophe and underscores the importance of understanding that Babyn Yar was a Jewish massacre in Ukraine.

Leonid Pervomais´kyi, "[Resurrect me, future, for a new]" (p. 175).
Ukrainian-language poem reprinted from Leonid Pervomais´kyi, *Khai lyshaiet´sia vohon´: z neopublikovanoï spadshchyny: poezii, proza, notatky, lysty* (Kyiv: Radians´kyi pys´mennyk, 1983), 27–28.

Leonid Pervomais´kyi, "In Babyn Yar" (p. 179).
Ukrainian-language poem reprinted from Leonid Pervomais´kyi, *Suzir´ia liry* (Kyiv: Dnipro, 1976), 23. The date of the poem is based on its inclusion in the poetry collection *Uroky poezii* (1968) which was one of the collections gathered in *Suzir´ia liry*.

Volodymyr Pidpalyi, "Babyn Yar" (p. 183).

Ukrainian-language poem reprinted from Volodymyr Pidpalyi, *Berehy zemli: iz spadshchyny poeta*, ed. N. Pidpala (Kyiv: Radians´kyi pys´mennyk, 1986), 105. The date is based on information in the collection.

The poem was published posthumously. According to Nina Pidpala, the poet was very interested in translating poets from Yiddish into Ukrainian and deeply involved in preparing, as an editor, books by Ukrainian-Jewish authors; in particular, he was responsible for the work on such poets as Ryva Baliasna, Iosyp Bukhbinder, Petro Kyrychans´kyi and Mykhailo Mohylevych. For more information on Pidpalyi and his encounters and work on the volumes of Yiddish-language writers, see Nina Pidpala, "'Nas khlib zhyvyv odyn, odni poily vody. Dilyly, iak braty my radist´ i pechal´...'," in H. Aronov and et. al., eds. *Dolia ievreis´koï dukhovnoï ta material´noï spadshchyny v XX stolitti: zbirnyk naukovykh prats´* (Kyiv: Instytut iudaïky, 2002), 198–204.

Maksym Ryl´s´kyi, "To the Jewish people" (p. 187).

Ukrainian text reprinted from Maksym Ryl´s´kyi, *Zibrannia tvoriv u 20-ty tomakh* (Kyiv: Naukova dumka, 1988), 19: 534–35. The poem was written specifically for an event held in the city of Ufa (now, in the Russian Federation) on September 20, 1942. The poem first appeared in print in Russian, in Ryl´s´kyi's own translation, in the volume of his selected poems *Slovo o materi-rodine: stikhi 1941–1942 g.* (Moscow: OGIZ, 1943), 29–30. The poem was not published in Ukrainian during the poet's lifetime and appeared posthumously in the nineteenth volume of Ryl´s´kyi's twenty-volume collected works, *Zibrannia tvoriv u 20-ty tomakh* (Kyiv: Naukova dumka, 1988), 19: 534–35. In his August 24, 1942, letter to Khaim Loitsker (1898–1970), a Soviet

Jewish literary critic and scholar, Ryl´s´kyi wrote: "I'm leaving the poems—I would be very glad if these were read on the 31st [of August] at the Jewish rally. Thus, I ask you—if they don't pose any negative reaction—to pass them where they are needed" (Ryl´s´kyi, *Zibrannia tvoriv*, 19: 201–2). The commentators suggest the rally took place on August 31, 1942, in the city of Ufa and all funds raised were dedicated to the construction of army tanks. The poem was read by someone else at the rally since at that time the poet was participating in the second anti-fascist rally of the representatives of the Ukrainian people in the city of Saratov (Ryl´s´kyi, *Zibrannia tvoriv*, 19: 534–35).

Ryl´s´kyi translated from Yiddish and served as the editor of several volumes by Jewish poets: Ryva Baliansova, David Hofshtein, Veniamin Hutians´kyi, Aron Kopshtein. For more on this poem and Ryl´s´kyi's relationships with Yiddish-language poets, see Nina Pidpala, "'Nas khlib zhyvyv odyn, odni poily vody. Dilyly, iak braty my radist´ i pechal´...'," in H. Aronov et. al., eds. *Dolia Ievreis´koï dukhovnoï ta material´noï spadshchyny v XX stolitti: zbirnyk naukovykh prats´* (Kyiv: Instytut iudaïky, 2002), 198–204.

With a witty smile, like the gray Moikher-Sforim: Mendele Moikher-Sforim [Mocher-Sforim] (pseudonym of Sholem Iankev Abramovich; 1836–1917) is best known for his literary works in Yiddish. Born in Belarus, he was orphaned early in life and traveled throughout Ukraine in the company of beggars. His early writings were in Hebrew; later he wrote novels and short stories in Yiddish. His most famous works deal with Jewish life in the Russian Empire; preeminent among the are *The Mare* (1873) and *The Travels of Benjamin the Third* (1878). Sholem Aleichem referred to Mocher-Sforim as the grandfather of Yiddish literature.

Like our Shvartsman: Osher Shvartsman (1890–1919) was a Yiddish poet. Born in the small town of Vil′nia, near Korostyshev in the Zhymotyr province, he grew up in the Kyiv province. In his youth, he composed poetry in Ukrainian and later switched to Yiddish. During World War I, he served in the cavalry and was decorated for bravery. After the war, he lived in Kyiv and participated in the publishing activity of the Kyiv Group of Yiddish Communist writers. After the pogrom of August 1919, he joined the rebel forces and was killed in battle. Several collections of his poetry appeared posthumously; he was crowned the model Soviet Yiddish poet. A bibliography of his works is included in the collection *Liderun Briv* (1935).

Iurii Shcherbak, "Basketball" (p. 191).

Ukrainian-language text reprinted from Iurii Shcherbak, *Fresky i fotohrafiï* (Kyiv: Molod′, 1984), 61.

In Kyiv, in Syrets: for Syrets, see Glossary.

Vasyl′ Shvets′, "Babyn Yar" (p. 195).

Ukrainian-language text reprinted from Vasyl′ Shvets′, *Dobryi ranok, Ukraïno*, ed. Pavlo Tychyna (Kyiv–Kharkiv: Ukraïns′ke derzhavne vydavnytstvo, 1945), 38–40.

A slightly different manuscript is housed at the Tsentral′nyi derzhavnyi arkhiv-muzei literatury i mystetstva Ukraïny (The Central State Archive-Museum of Literature and Art), Fond 949, op. 2, od. zb. 2, ark. 25, 25 zv.

For more information on the poem see: Mykola Tkachuk, Andrii Tkachuk, "Malovidomyi virsh Vasylia Shvetsia," *Literaturna Ukraïna* 12 (31 October 2016), 10.

over Podil, over all of Kyiv: for Podil, see Glossary.

Volodymyr Sosiura, "To the Jewish People" (p. 201).

Ukrainian-language poem reprinted from Volodymyr Sosiura, *Literatura i mystetstvo*, no. 19 (20 September 1942).

The poem was written for the anti-fascist rally held in the city of Ufa (now, the Russian Federation). Initially, the poem was published without a title, with three asterisks, in the newspaper *Literatura i mystetstvo* 19 (20 September 1942). For more information about the 1942 event, see the annotation to the poem by Maksym Ryl′s′kyi.

The newspaper *Literatura i mystetstvo* devoted a whole issue to the second anti-fascist rally of the representatives of the Ukrainian people. At around the same time, the Jewish anti-fascist rally took place. The Soviet Ukrainian Jewish writer Natan Rybak read Pavlo Tychyna's poem "To the Jewish People," as the newspaper reported, and the poem "To the Jewish People" by Maksym Ryl′s′kyi, read by the artist Romanov. Sosiura was present at the event and read the poem himself. There were also various Ukrainian Jewish writers who participated at the event and read their works ("Ievreis′kyi antyfashysts′kyi vechir," *Literatura i mystetstvo* 19 [20 September 1942], 3).

Volodymyr Sosiura, "Babyn Yar" (p. 205).

Ukrainian-language poem reprinted from Volodymyr Sosiura, "Babyn Iar," *Kyïvs′ka pravda* (December 1943). This poem, subtitled "Fragment" (uryvok), also appeared in Ukrainian in the Russian-language newspaper: *Sovetskaia Ukraina* 212 (27 November 1943).

Selected works on Sosiura's poem include: Tkachuk, "Malovidomyi virsh Volodymyra Sosiury 'Babyn Iar'," *Literaturna Ukraïna*, no. 39, (10 October 2013), 4.

Kurenivka, further on, and hung above the Dnipro: for Kurenivka and Dnipro, see Glossary.

In addition to the two aforementioned poems, Sosiura likely published another one, in 1946. Sosiura, like the writer Yuri Smolych, attended the court hearings of captured Nazi officers held in Kyiv in January of 1946. Eight German officers received death sentences and were executed on the central square of Kyiv. Although the full version of the poem is unavailable (most likely it was published in a newspaper or journal in 1946), below is an excerpt from it:

"За Бабин Яр прийшла година суду!
за нашу кров, за тьми свавільний гніт,
Це зла потвор, і безуму, і бруду
Рука відплати витягла на світ.
Судіть же їх, судіть в ім'я народу,
Від імені і мертвих, і живих,
Від імені життя і щастя, і свободи
О, судді праведні, судіть проклятих їх..."

Quoted from Vladimir Abaimov, "Kiev, ianvar´ 1946 goda: sud surovyi i pravednyi," *Zerkalo nedeli* 10 (March 15–22, 2001), https://zn.ua/SOCIUM/kiev,_yanvar_1946_goda_sud_surovyy_i_pravednyy.html.

Marta Tarnawsky, "In my life there also was Babyn Yar" (p. 213).

Ukrainian-language poem reprinted from Marta Tarnavs´ka, *Tykhi rozmovy z vichnistiu* (Philadelphia: Mosty, 1999), 85. Initially, the poem appeared in the journal *Suchasnist´*, no. 5 (1974):17–18. Later it was reprinted in the collection *Zemletrus* (New York: Slovo, 1981), 34–35, and *Tykhi rozmovy z vichnistiu* (1999), 85.

An English-language translation of the poem, by the author, appeared in: Olha Luchuk, Michael Naydan, eds. *Sto rokiv iunosti: antolohiia ukraïns´koï poeziï XX st. v anhlomovnykh perekladakh [=Hundred Years of Youth]* (Lviv: Litopys, 2000).

Pavlo Tychyna, "To the Jewish People" (p. 219).

Ukrainian text reprinted from Pavlo Tychyna, *Zibrannia tvoriv v dvanadtsiaty tomakh*, vol. 2: 1938–1953 (Kyiv: Naukova dumka, 1984), 264–66.

Originally the poem was published without a title, with three asterisks, in the newspaper *Literatura i mystetstvo* 19 (20 September 1942). Later, the poem was included in Tychna's collection *Den´ nastane* (1943). The poem was dated September 15–16, 1942, on one of the manuscripts that survived; however, in the newspaper publication it is dated only as August 1942. The poem was written for the anti-fascist rally that was held in the city of Ufa. During the event, the poem, in Tychyna's absence, was read by the Ukrainian writer Natan Rubak.

the iron voices of Solomon ibn Gabirol: Solomon ibn Gabirol (1021/22–1050/1058/1070?) was an Andalusian Jewish poet and philosopher. He published over a hundred poems, along with biblical exegesis, satire and other works. As a philosopher, he worked in the Neo-Platonic tradition.

of Ezra and Judah resounded—courageous Halev: Ezra, or Ezra the Scribe or Ezra the priest in the Book of Ezra, is a Jewish scribe and priest.

Courageous Judah Halevi: Judah ben Samuel Halevi (c. 1075–1141) was the premier Hebrew poet of his generation in medieval Spain. From the end of the eleventh century to the middle of the twelfth, Halevi wrote nearly 800 poems, both secular and religious. Halevi also defended the Jewish religion, which was then under attack.

Sholom Aleichem burst out laughing: Sholem Aleichem (1859–1916), the pen name of Sholem Rabinovitch, who was born in Ukraine. He first published Yiddish fiction in 1883 in the newspaper *Yudishes folksblat*. Even during his lifetime and, and especially after the death of the writer, literary historians canonized him as one of the "classic" figures of modern Yiddish literature.

among them, Osher Shvartsman shove: for Shvartsman, see the annotation to poem by Maksym Ryl´s´kyi.

Glossary

The Dnipro (Dnieper) is a major European river running through Russia, Belarus, and Ukraine. It flows from north to south through the center of Ukraine and passes through the city of Kyiv, dividing it into two parts.

Halytska Square is currently known as Victory Avenue, located in Kyiv. Its unofficial name, commonly used until the 1960s, was Ievreiskyi bazar (Ievbaza, the Jewish bazar). This was one of the places through which the Jews were forced to walk on the way to Babyn Yar.

Khreshchatyk is the main street in Kyiv. The street was completely destroyed during World War II by the NKVD and rebuilt after the war in the neoclassical Stalinist architectural style.

Kyiv-Pechersk Lavra or Kyievo-Pecherska Lavra, also the Kyiv Monastery of the Caves, is a historic Orthodox monastery which gave the name to one of the city districts.

Kurenivka is a historical neighborhood in Kyiv, known as a suburb of Kyiv from the first half of the eighteenth century. In the nineteenth century, Kurenivka, which was constantly growing, became a part of Kyiv. Now, it is located between the districts of Podil, Obolon, Priorka, and Syrets.

Kyryliv, before the Second World War, was a place on the outskirts of Kyiv where different institutions functioned. There was a psychoneurological hospital in Kyryliv, as well as the Jewish cemetery (which stopped functioning in the late 1920s), a hospital, and other institutions.

Luk'ianivka was a suburban town close to Kyiv that officially became part of the city in the second half of the nineteenth century. Its territory extended to Babyn Yar as well. Among several notable streets in that district, one may point out Melnykova Street (sometimes called Melnyk Street but now known predominantly as Melnykova Street).

It was along **Melnyk Street** in Kyiv that the Jews were forced to walk on their way to Babyn Yar.

Podil is a historical neighborhood in Kyiv overlooking the Dnipro. Podil is one of the oldest neighborhoods of Kyiv, the birthplace of trade, commerce, and industry in the city.

Syrets is another suburban area mentioned originally in the thirteenth and fourteenth centuries. Its name derives from the name of the river Syrets. In the late nineteenth and early twentieth centuries, Syrets was a place of privately owned homesteads, which were used as places to live or to run businesses. During World War II, the Nazis organized a concentration camp in that area.

Timeline

1941	Iakiv Hal´perin, "Laughter"
1942	Pavlo Tychyna, "To the Jewish People"
	Volodymyr Sosiura, "To the Jewish People"
	Maksym Ryl´s´kyi, "To the Jewish People"
1943	Mykola Bazhan, "Ravine"
	Volodymyr Sosiura, "Babyn Yar"
1944	Vasyl´ Shvets´, "Babyn Yar"
	Oleksa Iushchenko, "Babyn Yar"
1964	Leonid Pervomais´kyi, "[Resurrect me, future, for a new]"
1966	Leonid Cherevatenko, "Michelangelo"
	Ivan Drach, "[On June 22, 1966, at five in the afternoon]"
1968	Leonid Pervomais´kyi, "In Babyn Yar"
1972	Volodymyr Pidpalyi, "Babyn Yar"
	Marta Tarnawsky, "In my life too there was a Babyn Yar"
1974	Moisei Fishbein, "Ravine"
1975	Sava Holovanivs´kyi, "Melnyk Street"
1976	Ivan Drach, "A Kyiv Legend"
	Dmytro Pavlychko, "[On the edge of Babyn Yar]"
1977	Dmytro Pavlychko, "[Walking near Babyn Yar]"

1982	Igor Kaczurowskyj, "To Marta Tarnawsky"
1984	Iuri Shcherbak, "Basketball"
1989–90	Hryhorii Fal´kovych, "[From that horrible holy time]"
	Hryhorii Fal´kovych, "[Indian summer in Babyn Yar]"
	Hryhorii Fal´kovych, "[On the eve of holy Sabbath]"
1990	Abram Katsnel´son, "In Babyn Yar"
	Abram Katsnel´son, "Grandson's Monologue"
	Abram Katsnel´son, "Kyiv. September 29. Babyn Yar"
1991	Dmytro Pavlychko, "Requiem for Babyn Yar"
1997	Arkadii Anin, "Monologue of a Monument Never Built"
	Arkadii Anin, "Monologue of the Monument"
2001	Borys Dabo-Nikolaiev, "Tested by Tragedy"
2010	Leonid Cherevatenko, "The Gorgon Medusa"
2011	Leonid Cherevatenko, "1941: The Jewish Question"
2017	Denys Holubyts´kyi, "[The stones of my brothers and the sky of my sisters]"
	Marianna Kiyanovska, "[i would die on this street or on the one around the corner]"
	Marianna Kiyanovska, "[i even managed to grow during the war]"
	Marianna Kiyanovska, "[i will say it anyway i will accept it anyway]"
	Marianna Kiyanovska, "[these streets are already ruins maybe not all but already]"
	Marianna Kiyanovska, "[i've been getting together a collection for the last three weeks]"
	Marianna Kiyanovska, "[here is the ravine where hans does his shooting]"
2018	Valeria Bohuslavs´ka, "For Marianna Kiyanovska—in Response to Her Book *The Voices of Babyn Yar*"

Prior Publications In English Translation

Arkadii Anin, "Monologue of the Monument," *Volume Poetry* 7 (15 August 2021), https://volumepoetry.com/Monologue-of-the-Monument-Arkadiy-Anin.

Borys Dabo-Nikolaiev, "Tested by Tragedy," *Volume Poetry* 7 (15 August 2021), https://volumepoetry.com/Tested-by-Tragedy-Borys-Dabo-Nikolayev.

Illustration Credits

Illustrations

Poet Photographs

Bibliography

Poetry Sources

Anin, Arkadii. *Dotyk*. Kyiv, 1997.

Bazhan, Mykola. "[A muddy, clay green pit, ruddy void]." Translated by Amelia Glaser. *Odessa Review* 5 (October/November 2016): 39. https://issuu.com/theodessareview/docs/_5issue.

———. "The Ravine." *Babi Yar: The Source and Translations*. 2001. http://polyhymnion.org/lit/bazhan.

———. "The Ravine." Translated by Peter Tempest. *Ukrainian Canadian* (January 1977): 37.

———. "[Rust-colored cavity, green clay]." Translated by Roman Turovsky. *Odessa Review* 5 (October/November 2016): 39. https://issuu.com/theodessareview/docs/_5issue

———. *V dni viiny*. Kyiv: Viis′kove vydavnytstvo narodnoho komisariatu oborony, 1945.

Bohuslavs′ka, Valeriia. *Zemlia abetkovana: riznomanitni virshi*. Kyiv: Vydavnychyi dim "Buraho," 2018.

Cherevatenko, Leonid. *Vidkrytyi zvuk*. Kyiv: Radians′kyi pys′mennyk, 1982.

———. *Zakliate zalizo*. Kyiv: Dukh i litera, 2012.

Dabo-Nikolaiev, Borys. *Kyievu—Vsesvitovi mistu*. Kyiv: Zadruha, 2001.

Drach, Ivan. *Do dzherel*. Kyiv: Dnipro, 1972.

———. *Kyïvs´ke nebo*. Kyiv: Molod´, 1976.

———. *Orchard Lamps*. Edited and introduced by Stanley Kunitz. New York: Sheep Meadow Press, 1978.

———. *Poeziï*. Kyiv: Molod´, 1967.

Fal´kovych, Hryhorii. *Spoviduius´, use beru na sebe...* Kyiv: Ukraïns´kyi pys´mennyk, 1994.

Fishbein, Moisei. *Zbirka bez navzy*. Suchanist´, 1984.

———. Rannii rai. Kyiv: Fakt, 2006.

Holovanivs´kyi, Sava. *Synii ptakh: poezii*. Kyiv: Radians´kyi pys´mennyk, 1980.

Holubyts´kyi, Denys. "Ievreis´kyi tsykl." *Ukraïns´ka literaturna hazeta*, October 15, 2020. https://litgazeta.com.ua/poetry/denys-holubytskyj-ievrejskyj-tsykl/.

Iushchenko, Oleksa. *Vybrane*. Kyiv: Dnipro, 1977.

Kachurovs´kyi, Ihor [Igor Kaczurowskyj]. *Liryka*. Edited by Volodymyr Bazylevs´kyi and Olena O'Lir. Lviv: Astroliabiia, 2013.

———. *Svichada vichnosty*. Munich: Instytut literatury im. M. Oresta, 1990.

Katsnel´son, Abram. *Liryka*. Kyiv: Astarta, 2002.

Kiianovs´ka, Marianna [Marianna Kiyanovska]. *Babyn Iar. Holosamy*. Kyiv: Dukh i litera, 2017.

Pavlychko, Dmytro. "Rekviiem. Babyn Iar." *Vechirnii Kyïv* 95 (21 May 1991).

———. *Vybrani tvory*. Vol. 2. Kyiv: Dnipro, 1979.

Pervach, Mykola [Iakiv Hal´perin]. "Smikh." *Litavry*, no. 3 (30 November 1941): 2.

Pervomais´kyi, Leonid. *Khai lyshaiet´sia vohon´: z neopublikovanoï spadshchyny: poeziï, proza, notatky, lysty*. Kyiv: Radians´kyi pys´mennyk, 1983.

———. *Suzir´ia liry*. Kyiv: Dnipro, 1976.

Pidpalyi, Volodymyr. *Berehy zemli: iz spadshchyny poeta*. Edited by Nina Pidpala. Kyiv: Radians′kyi pys′mennyk, 1986.

Ryl′s′kyi, Maksym. *Zibrannia tvoriv u 20-ty tomakh*. Vol. 19. Kyiv: Naukova dumka, 1988.

Shcherbak, Iurii. *Fresky i fotohrafiï*. Kyiv: Molod′, 1984.

Shvets′, Vasyl′. *Dobryi ranok, Ukraïno*. Kharkiv, 1945.

Sosiura, Volodymyr. "Babyn Iar." *Sovetskaia Ukraina* 212 (27 November 1943).

———. "Babyn Iar," *Kyïvs′ka pravda* (December 1943).

———. "Ievreis′komu narodovi." *Literatura i mystetstvo*, no. 19 (20 September 1942).

Tarnavs′ka, Marta [Marta Tarnawsky]. "In My Life, Too, There Was a Babyn Yar." In Olha Luchuk and Michael Naydan, eds. *A Hundred Years of Youth [=Sto rokiv iunosti: antolohiia ukraïns′koï poeziï XX st. v anhlomovnykh perekladakh]*. Lviv: Litopys, 2000, 86.

———. *Tykhi rozmovy z vichnistiu*. Philadelphia: Mosty, 1999.

———. "V zhytti moiemu tezh buv Babyn Iar." Suchasnist′ 14, no. 5 (1974): 17–18.

———. *Zemletrus*. New York: Slovo, 1981.

Tychyna, Pavlo. *Zibrannia tvoriv v dvanadtsiaty tomakh*. Vol. 2: 1938–1953. Kyiv: Naukova dumka, 1984.

Research Sources

Abaimov, Vladimir. "Kiev, ianvar′ 1946 goda: sud surovyi i pravednyi," *Zerkalo nedeli* 10 (15–22 March 2001). https://zn.ua/SOCIUM/kiev,_yanvar_1946_goda_sud_surovyy_i_pravednyy.html.

Achilli, Alessandro. "Individual, yet collective voices: polyphonic poetic memories in contemporary Ukrainian literature." *Canadian Slavonic Papers* 62, no. 1 (2020): 4–26.

Anatolii (Kuznetsov), A. *Babii Iar: Roman-dokument*. 2nd edition. München: Posev, 1973.

———. *Babi Yar: A Document in the Form of a Novel*. Translated by David Floyd. New York: Farrar, Straus, and Giroux, 1970.

Anstei, Olga. *Dver′ v stene*. Munich, 1948.

Basic Historical Narrative of the Babyn Yar Holocaust Memorial Center, 2018. https://babynyar.org/storage/main/e0/ce/e0ced2fd93bcb8a9abbdeb5df828416f12fdac9eaf096d2766b54c989e86e48b.pdf.

Bazhan, Mykola. *Tvory v chotyr′okh tomakh*. Vol. 3. Edited by N. Bazhan-Lauer. Kyiv: Dnipro, 1985.

Berdichevskii, Mark. "Kiev sorok piatogo goda. Pamiati Iakova Gal′perina. Stikhi." *Kontinent* 136 (2008). https://magazines.gorky.media/continent/2008/136/kiev-sorok-pyatogo-goda.html.

Berkhoff, Karel. *Harvest of Despair: Life and Death in Ukraine Under Nazi Rule*. Cambridge: Belknap Press of Harvard University Press, 2004.

Bilenky, Serhiy. *Imperial Urbanism in the Borderlands: Kyiv, 1800–1905*. Toronto: University of Toronto Press, 2018.

Bilozers′ka, Olena. "Ohydnyi renehat chy patriot Ukraïny." *Ukrainskie itogi*. 2007. https://bilozerska.livejournal.com/21067.html.

Bloshteyn, Maria. "Olga Anstei: A Life in Brief." *The Postil Magazine*, November 1, 2017. https://www.thepostil.com/olga-anstei-a-life-in-brief/.

Borwicz, Michał Maksymilian, ed. *Pieśń ujdzie cało: antologia wierszy o żydach pod okupacją niemiecką*. Warszawa: Centralna żydowska historyczna komisja w Polsce, 1947.

Brandon, Ray and Wendy Lower, eds. *The Shoah in Ukraine: History, Testimony, Representation*. Bloominghton and Indianapolis: University of Indiana Press, 2009.

Burakovskiy, Aleksandr. "Holocaust Remembrance in Ukraine: Memorialization of the Jewish Tragedy at Babi Yar." *Nationalities Papers* 39, no. 3 (May 2011): 371–89.

Cherepinsky, Jacqueline. "Babi Yar." In *The Holocaust: Memories and History*, ed. Viktoriia Khiterer, Ryan Barrick, and David Misal. Newcastle upon Tyne: Cambridge Studies Publishing, 2014.

———. "The Absence of the Babi Yar Massacre from Popular Memory." Ph.D. dissertation. West Chester University of Pennsylvania, 2010.

Chornyi, Borys [Boris Czerny], "Literaturni svidchennia masovoho znyshchennia ievreiv u Babynomu Iaru." In *Babyn Iar: masove vbyvstvo i pam'iat´ pro n´oho. Materialy mizhnarodnoi naukovoi konferentsii 24–25 zhovtnia 2011 r., m. Kyiv*, eds. Vitalii Nakhmanovych, Anatolii Podol´s´kyi, Mykhailo Tiahlyi, 198–210. Kyiv: Ukr. tsentr vyvchennia istorii Holokostu, 2012.

Clowes, E.W. "Constructing the Memory of the Holocaust: The Ambiguous Treatment of Babii Yar in Soviet Literature." *Partial Answers: Journal of Literature and the History of Ideas* 3, no. 2 (June 2005): 153–82.

Czerny, Boris. "Témoignages et œuvres littéraires sur le massacre de Babij Jar, 1941–1948." *Cahiers du monde russe* 53, no. 4 (2012): 513–570.

Dean, Martin. *Collaboration in the Holocaust: Crimes of the Local Police in Belorussia and Ukraine, 1941–1944*. New York: Macmillan Press/St. Martin's Press, 2008.

Desbois, Father Patrick. *The Holocaust by Bullets: A Priest's Journey to Uncover the Truth Behind the Murder of 1.5 Million Jews*. New York: Palgrave Macmillan, 2009.

Dmiterko, L. [Liubomyr Dmyterko], "Sostoianie i zadachi teatral´noi i literaturnoi kritiki na Ukraine." *Literaturnaia gazeta* 20 (9 March 1949).

Dovzhenko, Oleksandr. *Shchodennykovi zapysy, 1939–1956 [Dnevnikovye zapisi. 1939–1956]*. Edited by V. V. Zabrodin, E. Ia. Margolit. Kharkiv: Folio, 2013.

Dzyuba, Ivan. "On the Twenty-Fifth Anniversary of the Murders in Baby Yar." In *Polin: Studies in Polish Jewry*. Vol. 26: *Jews and Ukrainians*, ed. Yohanan Petrovsky-Shtern and Anthony Polonsky. Littman Library of Jewish Civilization, 2014.

Fedorovs´kyi, D. "Bab'iachyi iar (V maisterni khudozhnyka V. Ochynnikova)." *Radians´ke mystetstvo* (30 July 1947).

Fridman, Lev. "In Search of Mykola Bazhan's Legacy on The Eve of Babyn Yar Commemorations." *Odessa Review* 5 (October/November 2016): 34–45, https://issuu.com/theodessareview/docs/_5issue.

Gershenson, Olga. *The Phantom Holocaust: Soviet Cinema and Jewish Catastrophe*. New Brunswick, New Jersey: Rutgers University Press, 2013.

Grose, Peter. "Boys of Kiev Play Ball on Babi Yar." *New York Times* (June 26, 1966), L5.

"Historian Timothy Snyder: Babi Yar A Tragedy For All Ukrainians," *Radio Free Europe/Radio Liberty*, September 29, 2016. https://www.rferl.org/a/ukraine-babi-yar-historian-snyder-tragedy-for-all/28022569.html.

Hrynevych, Vladyslav and Pavlo-Robert Magochii [Paul Robert Magosci], eds. *Babyn Iar: istoriia i pam'iat´*. Kyiv: Dukh i litera, 2016.

Humenna, Dokiia. *Khreshchatyi iar (Kyiv 1941–43): Roman-khronika.* New York: Slovo, 1956.

Hundorova, Tamara. *The Post-Chornobyl Library: Ukrainian Postmodernism of the 1990s*. Translated by Sergiy Yakovenko. Boston: Academic Studies Press, 2019.

Ianovs´kyi, Iurii. *Vybrane*. Kyiv: Derzhavne vydavnytstvo khudozhn′oï literatury, 1949.

"Ievreis´kyi antyfashysts´kyi vechir." *Literatura i mystetstvo* 19 (20 September 1942).

Kaplan, Iurii, ed. *Ekho Bab'ego Iara: poeticheskaia antologiia*. Kiev: Rif, 1991.

———, ed. *Vidlunnia Babynoho Iaru: poetychna antolohiia*, introduction by Ivan Dziuba, 2nd edition. Kyiv: Iuh, 2001.

———, ed. *Vidlunnia Babynoho Iaru: poetychna antolohiia*, introduction by Ivan Dziuba, preface by Oleksandr Moroz, 3rdedition. Kyiv: Iuh, 2006.

Khazan, Liubov´. *Saga o rytsariakh Bab'ego Iara: Il´ia Erenburg, Lev Ozerov, Pavel Antokol´skii, Viktor Nekrasov, Ada Rybachuk i Vladimir Mel´nichenko, Evgeni Evtushenko, Anatolii Kunetsov, Naum Korzhavin i drugie*. Kiev; Erusalim: ILEKNIF, 2018.

Khiterer, Victoria. *Jewish City or Inferno of Russian Israel? A History of the Jews in Kiev before February 1917*. Boston: Academic Studies Press, 2016.

Kiebuzinski, Ksenya and Alexander J. Motyl, eds. *The Great West Ukrainian Prison Massacre of 1941: A Sourcebook*. Amsterdam: Amsterdam University Press, 2016.

Klid, Bohdan and Alexander J. Motyl, eds. *Holodomor Reader: A Sourcebook on the Famine of 1932–1933 in Ukraine*. Toronto: Canadian Institute for Ukrainian Studies Press, 2012.

Korey, William. "A Monument over Babi Yar?" In *The Holocaust in the Soviet Union: Studies and Sources on the Destruction of the Jews in the Nazi-occupied Territories of the USSR, 1941–45*, ed. Lucjan Dobroszycki and Jeffrey Gurock, 61–74. New York: M. E. Sharpe, 1993.

Korzhavin, Naum. "V soblaznakh krovavoi epokhi." *Novyi mir* 8 (1992): 130–93.

Kostenko, Lina. *Poezii*, ed. Osyp Zinkevych. Ukraïns´ke Vydavnytstvo Smoloskyp im. V. Symonenka, 1969.

Kreyd, Vadim. "Ainstei, Olga Nikolaevna." In *Dictionary of Russian Women Writers*, ed. B. L. Bessonov, Marina Ledkovskaia-Astman, Charlotte Rosenthal, Mary Fleming Zirin, 33–35. Greenwood Publishing Group, 1994.

Kucheruk, Oleksandr. "Mykola Pervach: '... i vy pochuiete shche znovu i znovu prorochu movu." *Orhanizatsiia ukraïns´kykh natsionalistiv*. October 10, 2016. http://kmoun.info/2016/10/10/oleksandr-kucheruk-mikola-pervach-i-vi-pochuyete-shhe-znovu-i-znovu-poetovu-prorochu-movu/.

Ilya Kukulin, "Afterword." In *Written in the Dark: Five Poets in the Siege of Leningrad*, ed. Polina Barskova. Brooklyn: Ugly Duckling Presse, 2016.

Lazitskaia, I. "...Pravo na nastoiashchuiu zhizn..." *Raduga* 12 (2006): 147–69.

Mankoff, Jeff. "Babi Yar and the Struggle for Memory, 1944–2004." *Ab Imperio*, no. 2 (2004): 393–415.

Lekht, Naya. "Narratives of Return: Babii Iar and Holocaust Literature in the Soviet Union." Ph.D. dissertation. University of California, Los Angeles, 2013.

Levitas, Il´ia. *Babii Iar: kniga pamiati*. Kiev: Stal´, 2005.

———. *Babii Iar: spasiteli i spasennye*. Kiev: Tipografiia "Izdatel´s´tvo Stal´, 2005.

———. *Babii Iar v serdtse: poeziia*. Kyiv: Holovna spetsializovana redaktsiia literatury movany natsional'nykh menshyn, 2001).

———. *Pamiat´ Bab´ego Iara: vospominaniia, dokumenty*. Kiev: Evreiskii sovet Ukrainy: Fond "Pamiat´ Bab´ego Iara," 2001.

———. *Pravedniki Bab´ego Iara*. Kiev: Evreiskii sovet Ukrainy; Fond "Pamiat´ Bab´ego Iara," 2001.

Lower, Wendy. *Nazi Empire-Building and the Holocaust in Ukraine*. Chapel Hill: University of North Carolina Press, 2005.

Meir, Natan M. *Kiev, Jewish Metropolis: A History, 1859–1914*. Indiana University Press, 2010.

Miłosz, Czesław. *New and Collected Poems, 1931–2001*. New York: Ecco Press, 2003.

Naimark, Norman M. "The many lives of Babi Yar." *Hoover Digest*, no. 2 (Spring 2017): 176–186.

Petrowskaja, Katja. *Maybe Esther: A Family Story*. Translated by Sheila Frisch. New York: Harper, 2018.

Petrovsky-Shtern, Yohanan. *Anti-Imperial Choice*. New Haven: Yale University Press, 2009.

———. "A Paradigm-Changing Day: Jews, Ukrainians, and the 25th Anniversary of the Babyn Yar," a Petryshyn Memorial Lecture delivered at the Ukrainian Research Institute at Harvard University, March 10, 2021.

Pidpala, Nina. "'Nas khlib zhyvyv odyn, odni poily vody. Dilyly, iak braty my radist′ i pechal′...'" In In *Dolia ievreis′koï dukhovnoï ta material′noï spadshchyny v XX stolitti: zbirnyk naukovykh prats′*, eds. H. Aronov et. al., 198–204. Kyiv: Instytut iudaïky, 2002.

Pilnik, Shay Arie. "The Representation of Babi Yar in Soviet Russian and Yiddish Literature." Ph.D. dissertation, The Jewish Theological Seminary of America, 2013.

Portnov, Andrii. "Viina. Kyïv. Shchodennyk." In Viktoriia Kolosova, *Kyïvs'kyi shchodennyk. 1940–1945*, eds. Olesia Lazarenko and Andrii Portnov. Kharkiv: Vydavnytstvo "Prava liudyny," 2021.

"Prishelets z togo sveta. Rasskaz khudozhnika Feliksa Zinov′vicha Gitermana." In *Neizvestnaia "Chernaia kniga." Materialy k "Chernoi knige" pod redaktsiei Vasiliia Grossmana i Il′i Erenburga*, ed. Il′ia Al′tman. Moscow: AST; Corpus, 2015.

Rapson, Jessica. *Topographies of Suffering: Buchenwald, Babi Yar, Lidice*. New York: Berghahn, 2017.

Roskies, David G. and Naomi Diamant. *Holocaust Literature: A History and Guide*. Boston: Brandeis University Press, 2012.

"Shchodennyk Niny Herasymovoï—meshkanky okupovanoho Kyieva." Natsional´nyi muzei istoriï Ukraïny u Druhii svitovii viini. March 2016.

Sheldon, Richard. "The Transformations of Babi Yar." In *Soviet Society and Culture. Essays in Honor of Vera S. Dunham*, ed. Terry L. Thompson and Richard Sheldon. Boulder and London: Westview Press, 1988.

Shkandrij, Myroslav. "Dokia Humenna's Depiction of the Second World War and the OUN in *Khreshchatyi iar*: How Readers Responded." *East/West: Journal of Ukrainian Studies* 3, no. 1 (2016): 89–109.

———. "Dokiia Humenna's Representation of the Second World War in Her Novel and Diary." *Harvard Ukrainian Studies* 32/33, part 2: ЖНИВА: Essays Presented in Honor of George G. Grabowicz on His Seventieth Birthday (2011–2014): 665–679.

———. *Jews in Ukrainian Literature*. New Haven: Yale University Press, 2009.

———. *Ukrainian Nationalism: Politics, Ideology, and Literature, 1929–1956*. New Haven: Yale University Press, 2015.

Shrayer, Maxim D. *I Saw It: Ilya Selvinsky and the Legacy of Bearing Witness to the Shoah*. Boston: Academic Studies Press, 2013.

———. "Ilya Ehrenburg's January 1945 *Novy mir* cycle and Soviet Memory of the Shoah." In *Eastern European Jewish Literature of the 20th and 21st Centuries: Identity and Poetics*, ed. Klavdia Smola, 191–209. Munich-Berlin: Die Welt der Slaven Sammelbände, Verlag Otto Sagner, 2013.

———. "Jewish-Russian Poets Bearing Witness to the Shoah, 1941–1946: Textual Evidence and Preliminary Conclusions." In *Studies in Slavic Languages and Literatures. ICCEES [International Council for Central and East European Studies] Congress Stockholm 2010 Papers and Contributions*, ed. Stefano

Garzonio, 59–119. Bologna: Portal on Central Eastern and Balkan Europe, 2011.

———. "Lev Ozerov as a Literary Witness to the Shoah in the Occupied Soviet Territories." In *The Holocaust: Memories and History*, eds. Victoria Khiterer, Ryan Barrick and David Misal, 176–187. Newcastle upon Tyne: Cambridge Scholars Publishing, 2014.

———. "Pavel Antokolsky as a Witness to the Shoah in Ukraine and Poland." *Polin: Studies in Polish Jewry*, no. 28 (2015): 541–556.

Tarnawsky, Maxim. "The Literary Fallout of the Chornobyl." The Danylo Husar Struk Memorial Lecture at University of Toronto, May 26, 2006. http://lab.chass.utoronto.ca/rescentre/slavic/ukr/audio/StrukLectures/Tarnawsky-2006.mp3.

Tkachuk, Mykola and Andrii Tkachuk. "Malovidomyi virsh Vasylia Shvetsia." *Literaturna Ukraïna* 12 (31 March 2016).

———. "Malovidomyi virsh Volodymyra Sosiury 'Babyn Iar'," *Literaturna Ukraïna*, no. 39 (10 October 2013).

Weiner, Amir. *Making Sense of the War: The Second World War and the Fate of the Bolshevik Revolution*. Princeton and Oxford: Princeton University Press, 2001.

Yekelchyk, Serhy. *Stalin's Children: Everyday Politics in the Wake of Total Yar*. New York: Oxford University Press, 2014.

Zaslavskii, Ritalii, ed. *Bol′*. Kyiv: Raduga, 1991.

———, ed. *Piatnadtsiat′ poetov—piatnadtsat′ sudeb*. Kyiv: Zhurnal "Raduga," 2002.

Index of Titles and First Lines in English Translation

Titles appear in italics. If the title and first line are identical, the first line is listed.

Index of First Lines and Titles in Ukrainian

Titles appear in italics. If the title and first line are identical, the first line is listed.